BURNED BUT NOT BROKEN

For What Was I Spared?

by **Michael J. Nolte**

foreword by **Debbye Turner**

Indigo Publishing Group, LLC

Publisher	Henry S. Beers
Associate Publisher	Richard J. Hutto
Associate Publisher	Rick L. Nolte
Executive Vice President	Robert G. Aldrich
Operations Manager	Gary G. Pulliam
Editor-in-Chief	Joni Woolf
Art Director/Designer	Julianne Gleaton
Designer	Daniel Emerson
Director of Marketing and Public Relations	Mary D. Robinson
Distribution	Nick Malloy

© 2007 Michael J. Nolte

Printed in the USA.
10 9 8 7 6 5 4 3 2 1

Library of Congress Control Number: 2007929656

ISBN: (13 digit) 978-1-934144-16-9
       (10 digit) 1-934144-16-9

Indigo books are available at quantity discounts with bulk purchase for educational, business, or sales promotional use. For information, please write to:
Indigo Publishing Group, LLC., SunTrust Bank Building, 435 Second Street, Suite 320, Macon, GA 31201, or call 866-311-9578.

Dedicated to the memory
of
Cathy Isgrig

The sensitive caretaker of my daughters,
The unconditional and loving friend to my wife,
The affirming cheerleader for every venture I started,
The person whom the Noltes will always love
"This ------------------------------------ much!"

Cathy...by her death,
began a series of the most painful
and most gratifying experiences of my life.

I can't wait to hear her laughter.

" I never ask, 'Why did this happen to me?', but rather, 'Why was I spared'?"
— Michael Nolte

My family three weeks before the wreck. This is the photo that stayed in my hospital room to give the doctor's a roadmap to reconstruct my face... and also my life. (photo Isaac Alongi)

Table of Contents

Acknowledgments

This is the hardest page of the book to write.

My thanks are directed to those that have made this post-Burn Unit chapter of my life more tolerable. They have lifted me up when I couldn't bear my own weight...both literally and figuratively. Whether it be the weight of my own body or the weight on my soul, these are the people to whom I will be forever grateful

To Dave Quinly, my handyman, for using every tool in his toolbox (pun intended) to keep my house and store operational. When my castle became first my cradle and then my cage, he solved or repaired every problem that I could see but not fix. His dedication to my family is a gift that I can't calibrate.

To Bill Groner, the videographer who prepared the moving montage of news clips, photos from the burn unit and my homecoming that are used in every speaking engagement. His talents created a graphic, unbelievable, and yet very real glimpse into the life of a burn victim.

To Steven J. Heeney, the most patient and longest listening friend a man could ever have. He is the one with whom I can process every step of this journey. There have been a lot of miles put on our hearts with each other.

To Ron Adrian, the man who cares for my family almost as much as I do. He would do and has done anything he could to help Barbie through this and is a constant reminder of how lucky we are to have daughters who are best friends. That's our excuse for their parents to be best friends as well.

To the women of my life: my mother Shirley Nolte, my little sisters Sherry and Jennifer, my rock/wife Barbie, my rainbow of constantly loving daughters, Emma-Lea, Justine, and Caroline...I couldn't have made it through this without your individual gestures of kindness.

To my dad, Henry J. Nolte, the person Barbie aptly describes as "the kindest person I've ever known." His quiet support and constant presence was a calming factor to all of us, particularly to Barbie.

For the "right time/right place" combination of Pete, Butch, Rick, Jeb, Jim, you took the speaking engagement experience and started me both humbled and at the top.

For Pat Mehmert, the woman who represents the best of Chamois. She kept my mom calmed and me encouraged. In spite of her own crosses, she is never too busy to lend an ear or offer a prayer for the Nolte family.

To the faceless, nameless people throughout the country who prayed for me as they learned of the tragedy. I felt their prayers. I am the recipient of their prayers. I have learned from them the reality of the power of prayer.

To the people in audiences to whom I've been invited to speak and have taken the time to write to me afterwards. Hearing that I've touched their hearts by simply sharing my story reminds me always, the reason I was spared.

To my collaborators, Laurie Bollig and Gene Fox. To my editor at Indigo, Joni Woolf. To my literary agent, Bob Snodgrass. They were the team that shepherded me through this first-time experience.

And lastly, thank you to all the friends and the medical community who said, "You should write a book." Originally I had no idea of what or why I would write. I had no idea of how it could help someone. Now I realize that part of my commission is to share this story, this profound, incredible story of survival. Without the insistence of friends to do so, I would never have sought out the professional assistance I needed in the publishing world. This is a story worth telling. It is a life worth celebrating.

To God, for tipping my hourglass over and giving me this second life. I'm your guy as long as you need me here. When you send for me next time, I'm ready, but if we could avoid the chariots of fire this time...I would be grateful.

– Michael J. Nolte

Foreword

I am amazed at the passion and gusto with which Mike Nolte approaches life. The Energizer bunny could take lessons from him! Long before his accident, he had a zest for life and love for people that was simply infectious. I have never seen him do ANYTHING half-heartedly. As a veterinarian, I often relate to the world through animal references. In this sense, Mike is pure Border Collie; high-energy, dedicated, loyal, and unrelenting. Please don't misinterpret my analogy as an insult. I am not comparing Mike to a dog. I am telling you that I could always count on him, as a friend, confidante, shoulder to cry on, buddy to gossip with, and brother to lean on.

I have known Mike for almost half of my life. I met him eighteen years ago. It was not at all a chance meeting. I was on a mission and he held a position that was key to my goals. I was a third year student in the College of Veterinary Medicine at the University of Missouri-Columbia but I wanted to compete in the Miss America Pageant. As a student in the ShowMe state, I was eligible for the Miss Missouri system. I wanted to make it to the Miss America stage and I had to win a state title in order to do that. After a thorough investigation, I was told that the local pageant to enter was the Miss Columbia Pageant, mainly because the director would be an invaluable support in preparing me for the Miss Missouri pageant. That director was Michael J. Nolte. While I do not remember all the details of that first meeting (I would bet that Mike does!), I remember how he made me feel.

Mike was immediately warm, accessible, enthusiastic, polite, and friendly. I liked him right away. Even though I was an out-of-state student, he made me feel like I belonged. And for that I am forever grateful. It was not long before Mike (and his wife, Barbie) were dear friends to me. He took my calls, made time for me when I dropped by his shop, invited me to his home, and treated me like family. When I say that Mike treated me like family, I mean that he was brutally honest with me whenever he felt it necessary. Anyone who knows Mike knows that he does not mince words. So when he thought my appearance was less than stellar, Mike was unflinchingly forthcoming. I will never forget the day he said to me, "Debbye, I think you are pretty but I don't think of you as glamorous. That is just not you." I carried that bit of "flattery" with me for years. The point being, I never had to guess what Mike was thinking. He told me flat out. And I love him for it!

The space I am allowed for this foreword is not adequate to recount all the ways Mike has poured into my life. But I will say that whenever I needed him, he was there, no matter what. He prepared me for the Miss Missouri pageant (that worked out pretty well; I won). He planned a homecoming celebration for me when I returned to Columbia, Missouri, as Miss America. He allowed me to host a celebration for my family and friends at his house when I finished veterinary school. And on countless occasions, he provided a spectacularly appointed guest room and loving atmosphere when I needed a place to spend the night.

So when Mike was in that horrible car tragedy, I never doubted that he would pull through. I never doubted that he would recover. I never doubted that Mike would be Mike again some day. That's just who he is, an indomitable spirit. Perhaps because of Mike's career, a casual observer might look at Mike's life and assume that it (and he) is all glitz with no substance. We who love him have always known differently. And the accident only proved what we already knew. Mike is a man of substance.

I have had many soul-baring conversations with Mike over the years. He is the type of person with whom you feel safe enough to be completely transparent. I have always known him to be sincere. But now, since the fire, his words carry more weight. He talks of wanting to fulfill the purpose for which God spared him. He talks of his desire to help others, especially burn victims. He talks of his passion to encourage, motivate, and empower. And like every other task that Mike has ever undertaken, he will certainly do those things—and more. I don't think it was an "accident" that God allowed Mike to be tried by fire. Fire is a purifier. When it takes its full course, fire burns away the chaff, the frivolous, the insignificant, and leaves only what is pure. When Mike was burned, he was not at all diminished, because the fire could not burn the mettle of his soul. He was left shining, dazzling, and stronger than ever before. Yes, Michael J. Nolte was tried by fire but, hallelujah, he has come out as pure gold.

I am so proud of Mike. I am more proud to be counted as his friend. I love you dearly, my friend.

Debbye Turner
Miss America, 1990
CBS Staff Correspondent

ONE
Gravel and Fescue

The spring sunrise was soft and promising.

The task at hand was hard and filled with dread.

As I drove into the wakening horizon, I had two things on my mind – my dear friend Cathy, who had unexpectedly died the night before, and avoiding a speeding ticket. I had no time to be stopped. My already full "to-do list" had just reached overload. The new morning, radiant with gold first light and bright-eyed green landscape, belied my mood of having to plan an unexpected funeral in the next few hours.

I had stepped into that role with increasing frequency but all too close to home in these last few years. It was particularly hard just 11 months ago. Until just the night before, I finally felt like I was getting back on top of my game. Though my career of 24 years was that of a wedding planner, losses in my personal life had nominated me to work in tandem with funeral directors. There was a lot of overlap in planning weddings and funerals – music, flowers, attire, programs, church services, attendants/pallbearers, agenda of the event and, of course, family dynamics. It was hard to be emotionally detached, but I had to stay somewhat task oriented to be any good to the family I was helping.

If there was any solace and relief in my early morning trip down Interstate 70 from Leawood, Kansas, to Mexico, Missouri, it was that I could alternately consider what I might create for Cathy's funeral and what was already in place for the slate of weekend weddings of my clients Stacey Bograd, Vicki Cason, and Kim Corrigan.

I had met until 7 p.m. the night before at my store, Nolte's Bridal Collections, with Stacey and her fiancé Michael Howard. Impending weddings can be a source of great stress, but generally the rhythm is almost always one of happy anticipation. It is a gratifying profession in which I work. Even though it takes late hours sometimes, I know that I make a difference.

I had need for lots more hours on Wednesday, May 21, 2003, after I finished my visit with Stacey and hurried home for dinner with my family. I knew it had to be quick because I still had to press and prepare to deliver 110 white graduation gowns for the seniors of Notre Dame de Sion High School. Their big day started tomorrow with a 10 a.m. Mass at St. Thomas More Church. I would have the gowns delivered by 8:30 a.m. But as I entered the kitchen and heard my wife, Barbie, I knew something was terribly wrong.

Barbie was leaning against the counter, phone to her ear, her sobs defining the moment.

Handing me the phone, she said, "It's Cathy, Mike. She just died."

Stunned silence was my only response.

"Mike, it's me," I heard Cathy's sister, Charlene Finck, say in the receiver. "She died about an hour ago. She had a stroke."

"A stroke? Cathy's only 34!" My mind raced as Charlene spoke words that jumbled in my brain.

".........we found a letter that Cathy had written as she knew she was getting sicker with lupus," I heard as Charlene's words began to register. "She asked that if she died before you could plan her wedding, could you plan her funeral? She would like whatever you might suggest.

"I'm sure you're swamped with weddings this weekend, so I don't expect you to personally come, but could you fax me some ideas for flowers, the obituary, the readings, what to dress her in, the kind of casket she might like," Charlene continued.

"Charlene, are you using Arnold's (funeral home)?"

"Yes."

"We're not planning Cathy's funeral over the fax machine. I'll meet you there at 9 in the morning."

As I left the house at 6 a.m., I set my cruise control at 65. It would be a very full Thursday. Six hours of driving. I had absolutely no time to get pulled over for speeding. After almost an hour alone, in the quiet of my Lincoln, I could compartmentalize the grief of Cathy's death. I had to hunker down in "project mode." What kind of memorial would be best for Cathy? What kind of tribute could possibly be good enough for such an incredible friend? Such an amazing, loving, constantly giving person.

In the meantime, reminders and fleeting thoughts about the three "happy events" (the weekend's weddings) punched in and out of my scrambled thoughts. With all that was so upside down in my head, I couldn't help but note the peacefulness, the clear sky, and the serene beauty of the morning. May was the month in which I was married. In two days, Barbie and I would celebrate our 23rd wedding anniversary. But shouldn't Mother Nature be crying today too?

The reverie was broken by the severity of blue and red flashing lights in my rear view mirror. I glimpsed at my clock – 6:46 a.m.

It was the last few minutes of tranquility I would know for years. Within minutes, this serenity of nature was to be transformed into a searing explosion of hell. In one instant, it was a beautiful spring morning in mid-Missouri, the next, a violent Hades that would forever change my life as well as many others.

In a flash I was robust and alive, the next instant, I was near death. It was that immediate. I thank God, now, that my life was spared, but it was to become one filled with unbelievable pain. Pain reaching levels that caused me to wish He hadn't spared me.

I lived; the state trooper at my side did not.

1.8 seconds – or about as long as it takes to read this sentence.

That's how quickly the flames consumed us. That's how fast one's being can change, or end, in a blistering glint. I don't recall the pain, just the orange flames and the expression of confusion on Mike Newton's face as his life was ending.

His bewildered look I'm sure was a reflection of my own. The orange fireball rushed upward from the floor, past his waist, past the shine of his badge "799" before engulfing his head. There were no screams of pain, only the surreal seconds when his face turned gray, then black and shriveled like a sheet of wrapping paper tossed in the fireplace. Mike's face dissolved before me as my consciousness melted to black.

All I remember next is the distinct smell of fescue. I could not see, nor hear, but simply smell...the fescue. Why was I in this pasture? Was I dead?

The angel of death had pulverized my heart, first taking my beloved niece Micah and now our friend Cathy. Yet you shall not take me.

At this point I must say why I was compelled to write my story. I have chosen to recount my very worst moment and to revisit its many lesser worst moments in order to help those who have suffered like me. I am a burn victim. On the scale of pain and suffering, they don't get much higher than burn victims. We are exposed to a unique set of circumstances in our treatment and healing. And, truthfully, not many people live to tell about it, much less write books about the experience. Who would want to relive what is truly a horror like no other? Well, I do. I do because there is hope for those who suffer burns. I wanted to retell my story of struggle and recovery because I want victims and their families to know that you can reclaim your life. I wanted to give them a glimpse of what to expect and how to handle certain situations. But most importantly, I want to validate every emotion they are feeling, every bad day they have and each small triumph that gives them hope. I simply want other burn victims to know there is life to be lived. There is certainly a new definition of that life, but it's a life worth living nonetheless.

Six generations of Noltes have been born, raised, and died in my tiny Missouri town of Chamois, population 456. Though sadness had been a part of my father's life as his mother died when he was 10 and his father drowned when he was away in the Navy, never had the timbre of the present generation of family been shaken as it was in a single year beginning in mid-summer 2002.

It would be months before I would come to accept this trial fully. Perspective would come slowly, painfully, for all of us. Until that tragic June, my life had mirrored episodes of the Cleavers. I respected my parents, their values and morals. I treasured the friendships of my younger sisters. Dad was retired from Union Pacific Railroad and I connected "home" with the whistle of the train that passed through town and near my parents' house.

I was a good kid who got above-average grades and enjoyed my after school jobs at the drugstore and the butcher shop. I dated nice girls, had plenty of friends, enjoyed the company of many senior citizens and knew that I would be the first in my family to graduate from high school. Subsequently my sisters would do the same – only they graduated as valedictorians.

Voted "Most Likely to Succeed," I left for college the same day my baby sister Jennifer started kindergarten. The three of us graduated college as well, thanks to the sacrifices of my parents working with a single household income.

Armed with a degree in speech communication and photojournalism, I started working on my master's degree and began teaching high school in Boonville, Missouri. I loved the kids and they loved me. It was fluke to have as my students three children of the Zeller family – a freshman, a sophomore, and a junior. The youngest, Paula, served as matchmaker and introduced me to her older sister Barbie, then a junior at the nearby University of Missouri School of Nursing.

We married, she graduated as an RN, and I left teaching to start my own business of photography and floristry. We moved 30 miles to Columbia and shared one car for a long time. Her salary put supper on the table for that first year. Supper consisted many times of macaroni and cheese...period. It was on sale at IGA grocery for 31 cents a box.

Though we were both the first born, we became uncle and aunt before we became parents. After six and a half years, our first daughter, Emma-Lea Catherine, came into our lives and another colorful thread was woven into the tapestry of extended family. Reunions for weddings, birthdays, retirements, and holidays became the stuff of real-life Norman Rockwell.

We expanded professionally as well. Nolte's Inc. morphed into a wedding specialty business as I dropped photography and developed a bridal and tuxedo business. We built three houses in our years there and I enjoyed helping out on councils and boards at church and in the business community. I was named the Executive Director of the Miss Columbia Scholarship Pageant.

Three of my city level winners were consecutively crowned Miss Missouri and one, Debbye Turner, was crowned Missouri's first Miss America.

The business flourished and expanded, as did our family again, with the addition of Justine Elizabeth, two years younger than Emma- Lea. Our only source of anxiety was self-imposed when, at Barbie's urging, I built what I thought would be a satellite store in Overland Park, Kansas, an affluent suburb of Kansas City. It was 130 miles from Columbia.

The opening of Nolte's at Hawthorne Plaza though, was perfectly timed for the Kansas City suburban marketplace. The business was an instant success and required me to commute. I slept on a couch in the back room for 14 months before the entire family could re-locate. As the business expanded again, so did the family. Part of our re-location delay was the unexpected but thrilling conception of Daughter #3. Welcome Caroline McClain. As I sold the Columbia operations of my florist business and bridal store, we built a two-story Colonial and put up a white picket fence.

Fatal car accidents were something that happened to other people in the headlines of small town newspapers.

TEEN DIES AFTER TRAIN COLLIDES WITH JEEP

"Micah Starke, 18, of Chamois was northbound....as she approached the tracks....."

Or in *The Kansas City Star.*

MISSOURI TROOPER DIES IN FLAMING I-70 CRASH

Beyond the gruesome banner of each headline in the second paragraph of the stories were the names of the survivors. Both Michael.

Back in Chamois, the first Michael required suturing a scalp gash and was a pallbearer at his friend's funeral a week later. The second Michael, the one on I-70, was severely burned.

Life. Death. The distance between them is but a moment.

In my moment, I knew nothing except the smell of fescue. I was taken back to the farm community of my upbringing.

I was in a pasture. I could comprehend nothing else. Not even the events of 11 months earlier – June 30, 2002 – when my niece Micah also lay motionless, but not in pasture grass, rather in sharp gravel near the tracks of the Union Pacific.

Micah was everybody's daughter. Bright. Real. Pretty. She was one of those people with presence. She was the second child of my sister Sherry and brother-in-law Tom Starke. They had been married just eight months before us. Ashley, their oldest, was my godchild. Jordan was the only son and Caitlin, their youngest, is Barbie's godchild.

The Noltes and Starkes were similar families, forged by generations in the region. Sherry's children were like our own to us. As Micah approached her proms or homecomings, she had the privilege of gowns from my store just like had been offered to Ashley. She chose a coral dress for her junior prom and an olive gown her senior year. She wore the coral dress again for the golden wedding anniversary celebration for my parents in February 2002. She wore it a final time when we buried her four months later.

Micah excelled at everything she tried – drum majorette, 4-H Club president, varsity volleyball and basketball. She loved horses and riding. She volunteered at a local veterinary clinic and planned her future as an equine vet. She graduated as salutatorian of her class. In a month, she was headed to the University of Missouri to become an equine vet.

She spent most of June 30 at the home of my parents, just a mile from her own. It was not uncommon for her to spend several days a month with her grandparents and she often would nap there on Sunday afternoons. She left them about 4 p.m. and was joined in an afternoon ride by her classmate Michael Sieg as they discussed their futures as a vet and pharmacist respectively.

They approached an unguarded railroad crossing (no gates, lights or warning bells). It was within view of Micah's parents' house and just a half-mile from that of her grandparents. Micah observed a train stopped for a customary brake check and heard a loud horn blast. She and Michael presumed it was a signal that the train was about to resume its trip to St. Louis. Tragically, the parked train obscured an oncoming train traveling around a blind curve at 37 miles per hour.

Micah had been taught by her Grandpa Nolte to "Stop, look and listen."

She slowly coaxed the Jeep over the crossing.

The impact was sudden and intense, the engine striking the driver's side. Michael was ejected out the back window and Micah through the passenger side door. Micah suffered a massive head injury when she landed on the gravel of the rail bed.

"Mom, some man just called and told me to give you a message that your daughter has been injured by a train," Caitlin told her mother.

Sherry had no idea what it meant but she stepped outside to look toward the tracks and the crossing less than a mile from her house.

There was no unusual activity next to the train on the tracks. No sirens, no gathering crowds, but Sherry could only see one side of the tracks because of the idle train.

With Caitlin, Sherry drove back towards the center of town, stopping first at her parents' house. Both our parents came with her as she tried to determine the mystery call.

After driving to the crossing at the center of town where nothing was out of the ordinary she returned to the first crossing—the one nearest to her house. By this time, the cars of the stopped train had been separated in order for the emergency vehicles to get through. Sherry, our parents, and Caitlin saw the gathering crowd.

After telling Caitlin to stay in the car, Sherry and our parents ran through the separated train cars and saw Micah lying on the ground next to the track. From her vantage point, Sherry thought Micah was only unconscious.

Micah's eyes were closed as she lay on her back. Michael had taken off his shirt to shield her from the blazing sun. "Breathe, Micah breathe," Sherry whispered into her daughter's ear. No response. Just a gurgling sound.

Emergency vehicles arrived, including a Life Flight helicopter. Sherry located Tom on the farm and he joined them as Micah was loaded in. Her family started their trip to the University of Missouri Trauma Center in Columbia. Twenty minutes by air. Ninety minutes by road.

My sister Jennifer got the word first and from the river where she was boating with friends, she called us. Barbie and our daughters had just returned from a Zeller family reunion and we were enjoying the summer evening of reconnecting after a weekend apart.

When many weeks later I asked if she worried Micah might die en route to the hospital, Sherry told me, "Never.

"I thought when we arrived at the hospital, they would have her cleaned up and she would have her eyes open," Sherry said. "Even when I saw her on the ventilator, I was sure she was still alive. It never occurred to me that Micah could possibly be dead."

After receiving Jennifer's call, Barbie and I made arrangements for our girls and started the longest trip ever to Columbia. There were many calls back and forth for the two-hour trip. The first 90 minutes were frantic. Thirty minutes from the hospital, I heard Barbie ask Jennifer if anyone had come to talk to Sherry about organ donation. I nearly ran off the road.

"What are you talking about? You're talking like Micah's going to die!"

"Mike, this is really bad. I've talked to the ICU nurse who was one of my classmates."

We were like flint the remainder of the trip. I felt a sledgehammer hit my chest. No more emotion. No more conversation.

We parked illegally at the hospital and dashed through back hallways known only to those who have worked there. At the third floor intersection, I spied my sisters halfway down the hall. Sherry saw me coming and started sliding down the wall. Before I could get there, she was on the floor and all I could do was hold her. She didn't even look up when she said, "Mike, she's gone. My baby is dead."

In the deepest agony I've ever known, we huddled there for 20 minutes. Later when I embraced Tom, rivulets of tears marked his cheeks, still dusty from the soybean field where he got the call. My parents, Tom's mother and sister all were there, stunned, in a freezing cold, windowless, private room. About 90 friends gathered in the waiting room.

When the immediate family was allowed to see her, Micah was in a hospital gown. Swelling had started but her face and hands were still soft and pliable. Sherry and Tom of course were first. When Barbie and I stepped in, I wrapped my arms around Micah and whispered into her ear.

"Micah, it's Uncle Mike. Wake up. Micah, please, please wake up. Someone is going to think you are dead."

Barbie held Micah's hand and my own.

Micah didn't respond.

We were there all night.

It wasn't a surprise that Micah made a point to sign the back of her driver's license to be an organ donor. Most teenagers might not take the trouble or be too frightened to consider the prospect and ignore it all together. Not Micah. She got the transplant conditions correct, even if the organization had not.

"Pardon me if I'm not polished at this," began the representative of the organ donation network, "but this is only the fifth corpse I've worked with."

Sherry and I just stared at her in silence. "Corpse?"

That was not the last of the clumsiness. Micah's blood type had been bungled and potential recipients were notified, only to learn that they were not candidates after all. After the confusion was cleared up, the process inched forward. Sherry and I went through the checklist together of what would be donated. Tom was caring for their children out in the hallway and other relatives had gone to the waiting room. I'll never forget that time with my sister. It was excruciating. With Tom's blessing, Sherry signed the paperwork to donate Micah's corneas, her heart, kidneys, liver, lungs, and pancreas. I advised her to forego the donation of skin and bone as the image of such a donation made my stomach twist. That decision, based on myth and misconception, would later haunt me.

Because of the mix-ups, it took 30 hours and none of the family could bear to leave her side until the O.R. team was ready for the harvesting procedure. We never slept. I returned to Kansas City, attended Mass at 6:45 a.m., regrouped for an extended absence from my business, returned to the hospital and they were still there. I brought my funeral planning files with me.

"I want an extraordinary funeral for an extraordinary child." That was Sherry's only request to me. I took it from there.

They asked me to handle all that would come next. And I did. Planning is what I do.

As long as I was engaged in the mechanics of the event, I could stay just ahead of the grief. I burned full throttle and did not sleep for three days. Flowers, music, programs, obituary, pallbearers, clothes, phone calls, phone calls, phone calls. Because of the holiday, we had a six-day gap for preparation.

One of those mornings, I just lay in bed with Sherry and held her when she woke up crying. She showed me photos of Micah at last month's graduation party, and I chose one of her laughing for the program cover.

On the 4th of July, 1,200 people waited for hours to come see her, in state, in the church our great-grandfather helped to build. It was the church in which our parents married, our grandparents were all buried, most sacraments bestowed, and the Starkes also married. It was the church where Micah had been baptized. It was the church in which Micah had served Mass the Sunday she was killed.

I couldn't sleep the entire night before the funeral. Finally at 5 a.m., I drove up to the hilltop cemetery. Even in the pre-dawn, it was very hot. Watching the sunrise and the work of the backhoe begin at her gravesite, I finally found the words to write her eulogy. I finished at 8:30 a.m. By 10 a.m. it was 104 degrees.

With horses figuring so prominently in her life, a horse-drawn hearse was a natural choice. We walked behind the horses from the funeral home to the church. A drummer from the band she led played a muffled cadence and the church bell tolled every 10 seconds. As the procession rounded the corner, we could see more people standing outside the church than would fit inside. Her classmates carried her to her grave and at the conclusion of the burial service, coral and white balloons were released. They floated straight up to enhance the party she was enjoying in Heaven.

I returned to Chamois every weekend for two months to help with notes and organize the purchase of a new organ with the memorial donations. A month later it was installed and dedicated in her memory. Another ceremony to plan.

Our family struggled with the loss. I took my daughters to grief counseling. Dad, after much reluctance, began an anti-depressant. As a retiree of Union Pacific, he battled demons none of us had to encounter. Jennifer started drinking and Sherry and Tom started bickering. All predictable manifestations of unresolved grief. The Starkes began plans to build a new house in the country far from the railroad crossing and cemetery, both visible from their kitchen window.

Ashley suffered visibly the most. Her depression lasted most of the year.

She and her mother would get into ferocious arguments over ownership of Micah's things. Ashley would turn up missing in the evening only to be found at Micah's grave, night after night.

Three weeks after Micah's death, my high school buddy Ed Rost died of a heart attack. Age 47. Then Barbie's uncle Andy Bestgen died. Then her good friend Dr. Gouda, age 45. It was a tidal wave of death and funerals that summer.

Christmas was muted.

I have always invested a lot of time writing our holiday letter. "Nolte Novels" started in our early marriage serving as something of a journal for our daughters. All the original letters are bound in a Spode Christmas book. Until 2002 there was never a mention of sorrow, but it seemed to be a recurring theme of the newsletters to come.

At my suggestion that we change our holiday agenda, the family gathered at Big Cedar Lodge in southern Missouri near the Arkansas border. Two log cabins nestled in 16 inches of fresh snow for a week. All 13 of us. Micah's 19th birthday would have been December 23. That day a letter of gratitude from her kidney recipient was faxed to me there. That night we prayed the rosary for that family and for our own. We sang "Happy Birthday" to Micah and cried. Christmas morning, a candle from the altar of her funeral was lighted on the mantel and remained lighted all day. It was a hard experience, filled with softening gestures.

Puzzles, cards, and movies. Christmas dinner in a restaurant overlooking the frozen lake. We laughed (a lot) and slept late. The cousins never brushed their teeth and thankfully, they were in their own cabin. It was just what we needed. It was heavenly. More importantly, heavenly healing.

Winter ran its course and spring brought a sense of renewal to the Nolte and Starke families. You never get over that kind of loss. But you finally find the strength to start looking forward.

One of the bedrocks of support for the Noltes was our stable and loving relationship with our friend Cathy Isgrig. Cathy owned a large farming operation near Mexico, Missouri, three hours from Kansas City. Although we were separated geographically, our spiritual link was about to become even closer that spring when Cathy decided to convert to Catholicism. She asked Barbie and me to be her sponsors.

I first became acquainted with Cathy in the early years of my business. As the president of her college business and textiles club, she invited me to speak at their annual banquet in the mid 1980s. We clicked instantly. Later she inquired about an internship and had a proposal as to how it could work all mapped out. Following the internship, she stayed on as an employee during the rest of her career at the University of Missouri.

Cathy was a kid magnet. They all loved her, but none more so than Emma-Lea. Cathy started babysitting with Daughter #1 when Emma-Lea was two years old, and Cathy became a member of our family from that time forward.

When we moved into a new, three-story brick Colonial, we offered Cathy the lower level. She lived with us her senior year and was a nanny to Emma-Lea and Justine. Those girls loved each other so authentically. She made their Halloween costumes and planned tea parties for them. Studies came first, but she always made time for the girls each evening before bedtime. With my business commitments and Barbie working full-time as an R.N., Cathy was invaluable.

Graduating first in her department, she received lots of job offers and eventually decided to go with Sam's Wholesale Club in Bentonville, Arkansas. She started there as a fleece wear buyer. Though working way too many hours, she loved her job. On her trips back to her family in Mexico, she would often spend the night with us. We got to know her family well. Her father had died of cancer when she was 14 years old. Her sister Charlene and brother-in-law Jonathan were close to her both geographically and emotionally.

Always a high-energy worker, Cathy's vitality seemed to be sapped by the job in Bentonville. At first all of us attributed it to her rigorous work schedule, and Cathy regretfully decided to leave Sam's and come home to mid-Missouri. As she was making one of those last drives home, she was broadsided by a truck. The recovery was slower than it should have been and the cause discovered several months later. She was diagnosed with lupus, which resulted in attacks of inflammation and various allergic symptoms. That was what accounted for her energy drain, but none of us ever dreamed it was the sad beginning of a slow ending.

Complicating life for Cathy's family was Mrs. Isgrig's cancer diagnosis.

Upon her mother's death, Cathy inherited the farm. She and her older brother ran it, with Cathy doing her part of the job entirely by phone, as her allergies did not allow her to go outside unless it was below freezing.

Every summer, Cathy would host a housebound tea party for our girls, dressed in their summer finery. Cathy worked long hours to create games, gifts, and goodies. "How much do you think I love you?" Cathy always asked my girls, stretching out her hands six inches. "Is it this much?"

They would shake their heads.

"No? How much do I love you?" this time stretching her hands to 12 inches. Our girls would giggle, knowing the impending answer and actions and shake their heads again.

Now her arms spread wide, "No? Then it must be that I love you THIS much!" and she scooped them up in her arms and hugged them tightly. Giggles and love. Giggles and love.

Barbie and Cathy loved each other as well. After Caroline's birth, postpartum depression temporarily wrecked our marriage and home life. Cathy was the only one who got her to discuss her feelings and convinced her to see a doctor.

The Mass of Initiation to the Catholic faith was held in Mexico in the deep chill of February. The furnace blower was turned off to minimize the air-borne allergens. Cathy had shipped us special soap and shampoo to use before seeing her and we were asked not to wear deodorant, cologne or hair spray. With her slight cough, Barbie had to wear a surgical mask. Cathy as well wore a mask, much like she had done at her mother's funeral four years earlier.

We shivered through the 20-minute private ceremony, took some photos and recessed to Charlene's house for brunch. Though able to drive herself, Cathy wore a gas mask-like device and had an air purifier in her car to help her breathe. Later Cathy said it had been one of the happiest days of her life. She believed she was where she was always meant to be – in the arms of the Catholic Church and surrounded by the Fincks and Noltes. Though the Finck home was sealed, pumped only filtered air through its furnace, and had multiple room purifiers, the afternoon took its toll on Cathy. It was her last happy day.

From February to May, her health deteriorated. She was hospitalized in

April and never came home. The drugs she was taking for lupus thinned her blood and she began to lose circulation in her feet and hands. Barbie visited Cathy in the hospital and was troubled by her condition, but even after her last visit, Barbie believed Cathy was on the upswing.

It was after midnight when I finally got home from getting the dresses delivered for Sion's graduation Mass the next morning. Historically I am present, with a seamstress, for last-minute issues, but for the Class of 2003, I couldn't be there. I had been asked to plan another funeral.

Barbie was asleep by the time I returned from delivering my last load of gowns to the church that night, but before I could sleep myself, I assembled the items I would need the next day. One was my funeral file (too fresh from Micah's planning) and the other would be the clothes I would wear (more than jeans, less than a suit). Topsiders with rubber soles, olive chinos and a long sleeve blue chambray Polo shirt.

About 100 miles to the north in a small Missouri town, New Hampton, population 345, Paul Daniel also was tired from his day and finished some work on a bid for a new dock before getting to bed sometime before midnight. Like myself, he would be up early in the morning for a road trip.

To the east, in triangulation to Daniel and me, Mike Newton was also just getting to bed in Higginsville, Missouri. As a state trooper, he had to be up early to fill the 19-gallon gas tank of his Ford Crown Victoria before he could begin his shift early on Interstate 70.

The sun rose the morning of Thursday, May 22, 2003 – soft and promising.

TWO
Was It Worth It?

By anyone's standards, the stretch of Interstate 70 between Kansas City and Mile Marker 47 is dangerous.

That four-lane section into the Show Me State's flatlands is filled with speeding cars, tractor-trailers, and too many memorial white crosses that give testimony to its peril. The overworked route is a problem constantly under construction. The right lane is a washboard, the left lane hardly better.

Its two eastbound lanes and two westbound lanes have been beaten into submission between Kansas City and St. Louis.

The federal government has taken little initiative to make it safer other than to send its state troopers into the hazard with Ford Crown Victorias. It's a combustible combination.

I don't recall at what point I decided it was safer to avoid the bumpy right lane and switch to the left. Many motorists take the same strategy. Who would even think of getting pulled over for such a safety decision as this?

I know that shortly before Mile Marker 47, the flashing lights suddenly appeared in my rear view mirror. Seemingly out of nowhere, the Crown Vic came up behind me. I slowed down, signaled and switched lanes. The Crown Vic followed, both of us coming to a stop on the narrow shoulder just in front of a guardrail. I pulled over into the grass so far that my car was tilting and it was an effort to sit upright as I saw in my side mirror the trooper walking toward me. I wondered if I had given him a wide enough berth? I didn't want him to be harmed as he walked along the edge of the highway.

This was exactly what I didn't have time for today – a pull over. I needed to get to Mexico. I opened the glove box for insurance documentation and had my license out of my wallet by the time he was at my window. Regardless of the reason, I needed to get this experience behind me as quickly as possible. I kept my seat belt on and the motor running. I powered the window down before he could tap the glass.

"I bet you're wondering why I pulled you over," the boyish trooper said.

"It wasn't for speeding, was it? I had my cruise set for 65," I responded. As I looked up at him, I was immediately struck by how young he was and how small his face was – or was it just the size of the big hat?

"No, you weren't speeding. You were driving too long in the left lane. We've been having a lot of bottle-necking in this stretch, and I'm doing my part to break it up."

Thinking to myself how little traffic there was that morning, I kept it to myself and simply responded, "I'm sorry. I didn't even know it was against the law."

We were shouting our words as each semi tractor-trailer passed way too close. I was anxious not about getting a ticket or being late to Arnold's. I was anxious about the velocity of speeding cars only a few feet away from our bumpers.

"Where are you headed?" quizzed the trooper.

"What does this matter?" I thought to myself before replying, "Mexico, Missouri."

"Business or pleasure?"

Again, "What does it matter?" I replied however, "Neither. I'm going to plan the funeral of my friend. She died of a stroke last night. She was only 34."

"I'm going to need you to join me in my car." Looking up, I could see the gap between the sides of his shaved head and the hatband. Having been raised to respect the man "in the big hat," I reluctantly left the perceived safety of my own car to walk behind him to his. I can't claim to never having been pulled over, but I have never been asked to leave my car. Little did I know I was not required by law to do so.

All of this because I was driving in the left lane? Lurching out of the tilted seat, I barely opened the door so as to not have it struck by passing vehicles, and I inched my way along the edge of the highway. I just couldn't believe I was getting a ticket for this.

As I climbed in the front passenger seat, I noted that his air conditioner was on. Surely this wouldn't take long though. The clock in the dash read 6:50 a.m.

We made small talk about non-related topics as he pulled out his metal ticket- writing clipboard. I will always believe that his attitude toward me as a "law breaker" softened somewhat as he made the decision in his head to not give me a ticket but only a warning. I suspect that the reason for my travel must have stuck with him from the time we spoke of it at my window. A series of semis roared by. The Crown Vic rocked every time.

"I will need to see your license, though." His head was bent down as he wrote.

As I handed it to him, his head tipped up and he looked at me. Oddly, without referencing anything said before, he simply, quietly said, "I'm sorry for your loss."

These were his last words.

6:54 a.m.

Neither of us knew what happened next. We never saw the approaching truck out of our peripheral vision. Nothing could have prepared us for the violence and horror that enveloped us, becoming the moment. There was no sense of impact, no pain, no fear, no comprehension, no past, no future. Nothing.

Nothing but an orange rage.

I watched as he dissolved before me. And then I felt nothing.

The column of oily, black smoke rose thickly and swiftly. It could be seen for two miles on this pristine spring morning.

Sheriff Kerrick Alumbaugh, two miles away in Higginsville, could see the plume and began to hear the 911 calls. He raced to the scene. "It looked like the Crown Vic had been run over. It was completely engulfed in fire from end to end. Both cars were thrown off the highway."

By the time Alumbaugh and other emergency personnel arrived at the cataclysmic fire, Micheal Newton's life had already been extinguished but the flames that did so had not. Lying nearby in the grass I wavered back and forth; death to life, life to death, death to life.

In one single, careless moment our three lives, Newton's, Paul Daniel's and my own, had collided with such a force that the emotional, physical and legal ramifications would reverberate into our futures forever. It would become the subject of countless TV news reports and newspaper headlines across the state.

It is the kind of catastrophe that occurs when a one-ton pickup truck slams unchecked at 65 miles an hour into the rear end of a Ford Crown Victoria. There was an immediate and immense fireball followed by the compression of metal that seals all doors shut and the fate of humans inside. Soft tissue of human flesh incinerates in the 1.8 seconds it takes to reach 2,500-degree heat. Pain lasts a lifetime.

For the troopers working the scene, the carnage was highly emotional and personal. Although off the clock, trooper Brooks McGinnis rushed to the scene when he heard of his best friend's involvement of the I-70 crash.

"I thought it was a minor accident. I never expected to see what I did when I pulled up. Immediately I knew that Mike had to be dead," McGinnis said.

Troopers all over the United States are well aware of the explosive history of Ford's Crown Victorias. It is one of the few cars still designed with its gas tank between the rear axle and the back bumper, making it vulnerable to rupture and fire. Nationally, dozens of troopers and civilians have died in similar wrecks. Ford recalled and retrofitted model years 2001 and 2002 with a plastic shield to lessen the danger. Newton's was a 2003 model in which it was claimed that Ford fixed the problem. Still, many law enforcement agencies are leery of the vehicle. Some have been known to park in reverse at traffic stops so the front end is facing the oncoming traffic.

Trooper Newton, 25, had no understanding of what hit him in this fractured reality. Thus he felt no pain in the next three minutes that he lived. Nor was there for me as I now smoldered in the burning grass. My pain would come later and last forever.

Even Paul Daniel was not sure what happened when his truck's front axle broke on impact and yet continued for another 300 feet, tearing out the guardrail. Unhurt, he walked slowly back to the wreckage, passed my smoldering body and stood among the sightseers who were gathering on the slope. Reports tell me that approximately 75 people stopped to watch the flames that burned 40 feet in the air.

Each of us had begun the day before sunrise, each out of duty. Public safety for the state trooper, helping a friend's family in my case, and finishing a dock dismantle job for the third.

Was it possible that the aggressive trooper was trying to get a fast start on the day's competition? He might have seen me as his first "score."

"We often worked laser gun enforcement together on the highway," McGinnis said. "He was very competitive and we competed on a daily basis to be the first one to take someone to jail and to write the most tickets."

About the time Newton was pulling me over, Daniel took a call from his wife. Kathy chastised him for being gone from home on a day she didn't want him to work. At 6' 6" and 350 pounds, he was in no mood for nagging. He abruptly hung up. His right leg was sore and he heaved it up on the dashboard as he tossed the cell phone across the cab. The phone toss knocked his sunglasses to the floor on the passenger's side.

Daniel was also trucking down the highway on cruise control in the left lane.

With his left hand gripping the steering wheel, he bent over to pick up the sunglasses. The steering wheel followed his bending and the truck drifted across the centerline, through the right lane and headed for the shoulder and the flashing lights of the police car. As he bent his head below the dash, witnesses watched with horror as his truck sped directly to the shoulder where the patrol car and Lincoln sat unprotected. Inside were two men who never saw him coming.

The digits on the Crown Vic clock blinked.

6:54 a.m.

As I turned my gaze from the clock, I watched Trooper Newton scribble on his clipboard. As if in slow motion, Micheal Newton raised his head and our eyes met briefly, forever etched in my mind, in the last seconds of his life.

THREE
Cross Fire

Doug Mitchell had been in the business of accident investigation for more than 20 years when he got the call from Mike Newton's Troop A headquarters. Most of the time he can isolate himself from the tragic elements of his unique business. He is trained to uncover exactly what happened and sometimes who or what was at fault.

"There are days I can't get the stench of death out of my head," he said matter of factly. "But I know when I drive through the gates of my ranch (near Warrensburg, Missouri), I can either 'get lost' or 'lose it' and no one will find me. It keeps me sane."

Mitchell gets along well with everyone in the Missouri State Highway Patrol. He feels a special kinship with the foot soldiers. He is all but one of them in the brotherhood. He is also a member of Masters – an organization that financially assists families of troopers killed in the line of duty.

The call of May 22 rocked him – an accident involving Trooper Mike Newton. Though 21 years separated them, he and Newton had been friends. But business first.

Flying over the scene to get aerial photographs, he got a bird's eye view of the charred remains of the devastating wreck. Later, he was told that there had been a survivor in what he estimated to be the worst carnage in his career. Surely that was an impossibility. In passing, he heard the name of the survivor.

When he heard "Michael Nolte," his gut twisted again. "Who?"

He couldn't believe it. Just less than a year ago, we had become acquainted while he was assigned to do the investigation of my niece's death in Chamois. During that process we had become friends as well.

And now WHAT? Leawood...Chamois...Higginsville...Columbia...Mike Newton... Mike Nolte...Together?...On the highway?...Going where?...Doing what? It took him back quickly to the first time we met at my sister's house, just two weeks after the funeral. He now filled a very unique role.

He was dumbfounded by the irony that two disconnected friends could have been brought together by such catastrophe. Mitchell was the one common denominator to both families.

He went to work with double resolve to get every detail exactly right for what was going to be a major civil lawsuit. His expertise became a critical factor in the litigation against Ford Motor Company in the months that followed.

The details of what exactly happened after the impact were of importance to Mitchell and my attorneys but thankfully suppressed in my memory.

People had often asked if I felt or remembered the impact. The answer thankfully, had always been, "No." That was the truth...until *Seabiscuit.*

It had been six months since the wreck. Barbie and I decided to have a go at our "new normal." A movie would be a welcome distraction from the pseudo-hospital setting. A burn victim is neither a pleasant sight nor a pleasant person. Crabby, short tempered, and easily frustrated. Some level of pain is always present. The higher the level, the more miserable the patient. The more miserable the patient, the more miserable the family.

Seabiscuit had received good reviews and I had been given two copies to read while in the burn unit. Of course with a burned left hand, I couldn't hold a book, thus they didn't get read. Albeit in a wheelchair, off we headed to Town Center's AMC Theater to see the movie.

There is a scene that triggered it all for me. Red Pollard, the jockey played by Tobey Maguire, gets dragged with his foot caught in the stirrup. When the famous racehorse slammed him into the stable wall, the audience winced at the make-believe impact. For me it was not imaginary. It was Mile Marker 47 all over again in my mind's rear-view mirror. When Pollard's harrowing experience abruptly ended, the screen went black and I felt the impact of my earlier crash for the first time.

I became so upset, I couldn't stop crying or shaking. Thankfully we were in the highest row of seats and near the handicap exit door. Barbie rolled me out. I continued into the men's room, where I leaned over in the wheelchair and vomited into the urinal.

Trooper McGinnis recalled on a memorial Web site the time he was "bested" by Newton. Newton had radioed only one pull over, but ended up with taking three DUIs to jail at one time.

"I remember on one occasion, Mike called while he was en route to jail with three intoxicated drivers. I just about dropped the phone," McGinnis said. "I said 'You're full of it. How could you be on the way to jail with three people? I only heard you make one traffic stop.'"

Newton explained that he had pulled over one suspect and while standing outside the guy's car, nearly got hit by a slow-moving pickup. Thinking the flashing lights were for them, Mike explained, the pickup driver pulled over on the shoulder, in front of the first offender. The male driver switched seats with the female passenger thinking she was less intoxicated. The plan failed. Newton arrested both of them. McGinnis ended his reverie by admitting that Newton "won the competition that day."

Is competition what motivated Newton that morning?

If so, we ended up like Red Pollard. Getting slammed.

Only he's dead. And I'm vomiting in urinals.

When the "screen went black" for us, he grabbed my wrist as if somehow I could save him. I can still feel his grip.

How I wish I could save him.

How I wish I couldn't feel that grip.

I now understand the definition of the term "death grip."

Dave Bryan and Troy Brinkoetter, each trying to ward off low levels of life's discontent, were in separate cars behind Daniel's pickup. It was an unwitting caravan of people who in one moment would become linked for the rest of their lives.

Dave is a public information administrator for the Missouri Department of Economic Development. He hadn't received a raise in five years. His job required 2,000 miles a month on the road and he was late for a meeting in Jefferson City, the capital of Missouri. He had started from his home in nearby Liberty, an historic town just north of Kansas City. Twice he returned home for paperwork he had forgotten.

"Lord, there must be some reason you want me 25 minutes late, because now I am," he mumbled to himself, hurrying down the interstate.

Dave was in a funk...maybe a mid-life crunch, not crisis. Though loved by his wife, Susan, and his daughter, Machelle, he didn't feel vital to his family or his job. His faith, too, was in a bit of a desert. He felt disconnected.

Directly in front of Dave Bryan and a short distance behind Paul Daniel, Julia and Troy Brinkoetter were headed to the Veteran's Hospital in Columbia. Troy was going to see the specialist who had treated him for Gulf War Syndrome for a number of years. Only 33, Troy had suffered a light stroke three days earlier and was scheduled for a checkup.

Riding in the rear seat was their two-year-old daugther Brooke. Troy had been a firefighter with the Navy for 12 years before retiring to accept a position as chief of police of the hamlet of Strasburg, Missouri. Until now, very little had bothered this 6'6", 300-pound man. Troy, like Dave, was also feeling a bit ambivalent about his life. But life can change quickly.

Troy saw the pickup ahead begin to waft toward the center stripe, then into the right lane. Then the unbelievable became believable as it continued to slide toward the flashing lights.

"Julia!" Troy yelled, "That s.o.b. is going to hit......."

The sentence wasn't finished before the explosion shook the highway. Both the Crown Vic and the Lincoln were thrown from the interstate. The truck never slowed down before the impact and kept going afterwards as well. The fire consumed every inch of the form of the car.

The driver's side window creased like an accordion but never broke. Likewise, the driver's door was squashed to a quarter of its original size. Dave Bryan was the first to reach the car. He raced around to the passenger side where the glass had mysteriously shattered, but there were no broken shards on the ground or left in the frame. The black smoke was so thick he could see nothing inside but reached both hands in anyway.

"I don't know if I saw it or felt it first – a human shoulder," he would say months later in a deposition. "I put my hands under the arm and started pulling."

At 6'2" and 189 pounds, I was dead weight – or quickly on my way to becoming so – if Troy had not shown up mere seconds later. There were never any words of strategy between Dave and Troy, simply muscle and commitment to save a human life.

They pulled me out, unconscious and on fire. Once out of the window, they carried me into the grass and beat the flames on my face, hands and legs. They did so repeatedly as my clothing had been sprayed with gasoline and the field was on fire as well. I continued to reignite.

Most motorists slowed but then sped past the wreck. Dave and Troy continued to work the calamity. Few others bothered to get involved. Oddly... thankfully...a telephone repair truck stopped in mid-lane. The driver ran to the back, unlocked the doors of cargo hold and tossed out eight industrial fire extinguishers. After they clanked to the pavement, he sped away. I have never learned his identity. The fire extinguishers are what finally put out the blaze that was ravaging my body.

Troy grabbed one of the canisters and started swinging it like a baseball bat at the bulletproof glass. It was unbreakable. Finally the extreme heat and the explosion of ammunition from Trooper Newton's belt forced his retreat. Dave warned the motorists now using the extinguishers to stop spraying it uselessly on the raging inferno and use the last one on me.

"Cover his face and empty it on him," he ordered.

Just then I burst into flames a fourth time. The foam worked.

The rounds continued to explode from Newton's holster, blowing his right leg off his hip.

Shock caused all my senses to shut down. All senses save that of smell. I recall vividly the smell of fescue. My mind tried to put it together. I was laying face down in a cow pasture. Why would that be? Had the United States been bombed? Hussein wasn't captured yet and Whiteman Air Force Base was nearby. Would he have targeted the heartland of our country? Had I been shot? Was this the end of the world?

There was still no pain, but I did comprehend that something very bad had happened. I realized I might be dying. I prepared to do so. From deep within my gut came the words I had been taught since childhood – The Act of Contrition.

Oh my God...

I am heartily sorry for...

having offended Thee...

and I detest of all my sins...

because of Thy just punishment...

but most of all...

because they offend Thee my God...

who art all good...

and deserving of all my love...

I firmly resolve...

with the help of Thy grace...

to sin no more...

and to avoid the near occasion of sin.

Amen.

Since learning to serve Mass as an altar boy – a "Knight of the Altar" – I knew not only a few Latin responses, but also that this was the prayer Catholics were taught to pray when asking for total absolution for one's sins.

Raised in the Catholic faith at St. Charles Borremeo in Gladstone, Missouri, (until 6th grade), these words comforted me now 40 years later. It is the belief of the Catholic Church that the recitation of this prayer shortly before taking one's last breath ensures transition to heaven. I think I prayed it nine times.

Someone rolled me over. The shirt covering my face was removed so I could breathe and I could glimpse a surreal vision through the slit in my right eye that wasn't swollen shut yet. A man's shirt/towel/blanket/jacket was being waved up and down over me. Each time it was lifted, I could see its edges flaming.

"Why is that man's towel catching fire?" I thought to myself. "And why is he hitting me with a burning towel?" I had no conception that the flames were actually on me and transferring to the towel.

Trooper Bill Oliver was the first patrolman on the scene. His dashboard-mounted video camera recorder was automatically started when he turned on his flashing lights. The "dash cam" showed his easy walk up to the vehicle thinking it was an abandoned car that had self-ignited. But upon closer inspection, he sees the last inches of the patrol's decal on the driver's door and realizes it's one of his men. He sprints back to the car radio in a panic. As a training officer, he had been Newton's mentor.

"...I think it's 799...it's 799 and it's fully engulfed," Oliver is heard screaming. "He didn't get out!" In the background of the recording, Oliver's German Shepherd is heard whimpering at his master's tone of voice.

(That night the numbers of the Missouri Pick Three lotto would come up 7-9-9. It would do so again, exactly 30 days after the wreck.)

Lesley Loos had been an RN for 24 years and a flight nurse since 2001. She and Paul Langlotz, the paramedic, were both dispatched seven minutes after the 911 call came in to their Kansas City base. They got details on the way to the crash site. It would be a "hot landing" (the rotor would not turn off) and would have to be directly on the interstate. The highway had been shut down in both directions by this time. They knew going in it was going to be bad. Burn victims requiring Life Flight seldom made it to the hospital.

"...I firmly resolve...

with the help of Thy grace,

to sin no more...

and to avoid the near occasion of sin.

Amen."

I expected to be dead at any time, but I didn't think I was.

If that was the case, I would keep praying.

The rosary is another Catholic tradition that comes easily as my favorite form of prayer. I have been a part of a group that prays it almost every Tuesday evening for nearly 10 years. I keep a rosary in my console and pray it while I'm driving. It's an easy "stop and start" set of prayers that comprise 50 Hail Marys, five Our Fathers and five Glory Bes. It ends with the Hail Holy Queen, which I have down pat, but it's the beginning prayer, The Creed, that trips me up every time. I can only get through it with either a cheat sheet or if I'm standing next to someone who leads.

I decided to pray the rosary until something happened. I knew though that I would blow the opening prayer but felt that God would understand if I just jumped over it and went, in my head, to the next prayer bead – The Lord's Prayer. The mantra of the rosary is calming. Its power is proven to me over and over again.

Apparently praying out loud at this point, I began to hear an echo. Was it in my head?

Was it another human?

Not a human?

Human indeed, Ron Hicks, the son of a minister, had stopped to help but seeing there was nothing to be done now except wait for the helicopter, he heard me praying and knelt in the grass and prayed aloud with me.

He said in his deposition, "There was nothing I could do except say The Lord's Prayer with him. He had flesh sliding off his feet and legs, but it seemed to comfort him to pray." (Ron's praying with me was the only sound I could register in the field. All other conversations were just me talking to someone, not able to hear their answer. I was deaf in my left ear for eight months.)

My rubber-soled shoes had melted off my feet and taken my soles with them. My socks and pants were burned away as was part of my shirt. I felt someone cut off the remainder of my shirt. They ripped off my undershirt and then I felt the blade at my hip as it cut the waistband of my underwear. In a swift motion, a hand reached between my legs and pulled off what little clothing I had left. Even in that state of distress, I recall thinking "Oh great. Not only am I laying in a cow pasture, but I'm laying buck naked in a cow pasture – on my back!"

A spine board was wedged under my back and straps buckled across my bare torso. "On three," the paramedics said. "One... two... three..."

I felt them running through the fields bumping along until I was slid onto a flat hard surface (later determined to be a local ambulance that served as the holding room until the helicopter arrived.) "We're going to take good care of you. Hang on. Stay with us."

I slipped in and out of consciousness. I had no willingness to neither hang on nor let go. I was suspended in space and time. I didn't care. The pain was starting to lift me off the spine board.

Dying probably never happens the way we think it will. When I had a clear stream of thought, I fully imagined experiencing God and Heaven momentarily. It couldn't come fast enough now, as the pain caused me to buck against the straps holding me down.

They transferred me out of the ambulance, ran the gurney down the highway and slid me into the helicopter. The chopper had been on the ground only three minutes. The transfer was complete. It was the last time Dave and Troy were to see me for two years as I was shoved aboard Life Flight Eagle, unconscious, naked and charred. I never felt the ascent.

Over the propeller noise, I heard Leslie Loos explain, "We're being diverted. We're taking you to Columbia. KU (the University of Kansas Hospital) is full."

I tried to be conversational, "That's okay. We used to live in Columbia. For 13 years."

While I'm talking of everything and nothing, the medics are frantically working on me. They're checking my airway and listening for hoarseness in my voice. No soot in my mouth or throat, which is good. All facial hair has been burned off; eyebrows, eye lashes, whiskers, nasal hair – not a good thing.

"What did you do in Columbia?" Leslie asked.

"I owned a florist business there. Still enjoy landscaping," I answered, writhing in agony. Great agony.

"I love flowers too," she answered back, stunned by this patient interaction, especially when she could see the depth of the burns. What was happening? How could he be so casual? Odd.

"On a scale of one through 10," she decided to ask me, "10 being the highest, how would you rate your pain?"

"Ten," I finally screamed. (It was actually higher, but 10 was the highest option she gave me.)

Then the bottom fell out. Gone was my heart rate. Gone was my blood pressure. Finally. No pain.

Conversation and sensibility trickled away. They were quickly replaced with a sentiment, a feeling, a euphoria of serenity. How does one later describe complete spiritual tranquility without drawing snickers or rolled eyes? How does one put into words what we trust God to give us in afterlife?

I can only answer through my own experience, mostly inadequate are the words I use. What I can relate is that it was not unlike those who also have described the near-death phenomenon. I offer no hesitation, nor qualification to what I experienced during my span of unconsciousness. I simply tell the truth. For those who believe, they believe. For those who don't, they can refute it or discount it.

I began my ascension to God.

It was unlike anything I had experienced before. It was wonderful; it was pure contentment.

I'm a skeptic myself. How much is suggested? How much is real? Do you feel you're going "up" to heaven simply because it's always been referred to as "high in the heavens" or to God as "the man upstairs?"

Nonetheless, the sensation was exactly that – of floating up. I didn't realize at the time that it was heaven to which I was floating. It didn't matter. The transition was so pleasant that I wasn't anxious for a destination.

There was no weight to my body. No "pulling" me up. No "pushing" me up either. Simply floating. Completely weightless. Completely pain free. I had no ability to guide the ascent, to slow it down or speed it up. It was just happening.

And there was light.

Here I'm really at a loss of adjectives to describe the quality of that light. It was brilliant and yet glowing. (How can that be? Those are two different kinds of light.)

It was easy on the eyes and yet the clearest light I've ever seen.

There was definitely a tunnel, a pathway, a tube-like, soft-sided structure that seemed to be made personally for my trip. It retrospect, it was as if this channel had never been utilized before. Could it be that God really does create a plan for each of us – one that includes the tunnel that brings us directly from where we die on earth to the gates of heaven? Regardless of where that last breath is drawn, the tunnel is there. Has it been there all my life? Or was it just created in that instant, when I stopped breathing?

The sides of the tunnel were not solid or thick and yet I couldn't see through it. And it was soft. Though I never touched it, the medium of which it was made was like that of cotton and yet not formed into balls or walls. It just was. The fibers of this cotton were sparkling with tiny flecks, like the sugar crystals on cotton candy. The walls were glowing, shining as if there was stronger exterior light on the outside of the tunnel.

Occasionally there would be a gap in the tunnel and I could peek out and see the space through which I was passing.

The space had no horizon. No interruptions. It was all there was. White, light, clear, space. The only movement was that of white shapes of a marshmallow-y like substance. I registered that it reminded me of the Lava lamps of the '70s that had non-specific globs of color that floated up and down in the lighted globe. It was like that.

And then I heard her.

I have read since that as hospice patients are experiencing their slow shutting down of senses and bodily functions, they sense that someone from "the other side" comes to escort them to heaven. That was not my case. Maybe it was too sudden. I never saw anyone. But I did hear Micah.

I heard her laughing. Heartily. Authentically. Laughing like she did whe she stomped snow off her boots that Christmas morning, arriving for the holidays and exclaiming, "Uncle Mike, I just love all this glitz," referring to the decorations that only a former florist would go to the trouble to install.

She shook the snow out of her hair and hugged me. Micah was my kid. I'll never forget that moment. Her joy. Her pleasure to be with us. Her laughter. And now I was hearing it again. It had been almost a year.

She laughed loud enough that I could hear her, but always just out of sight. She was always just around the corner. The next bend. If anything was propelling me to move faster, it was my excitement in seeing her again. The higher I floated, the higher yet, she laughed.

I never saw Cathy. I jokingly say that having just been in heaven herself, less than 24 hours, she was too busy getting settled in to come back down for me.

I also never saw some of the things that people attribute to this crossing over. I never saw gates, a river, a threshold, a valley. I never saw scenes from my life flash before me.

I never saw God. But I knew that was going to happen.

Man, but did I know that was going to happen!

To give a sense of how euphoric this transition is for the one in the experience, I even thought of Barbie and the girls. I gratefully realized that I had protected my family with adequate life insurance. It would take care of them financially. God would take care of them emotionally. They were going to be okay even with me away. And I love my girls. That's how much stronger is the happiness of dying. The new life that awaited me was greater than the one I had enjoyed so much on earth...and I had had a wonderful life.

Then it changed.

Abruptly.

After seeing back into the helicopter and comprehending that the corpse they were covering with a warming blanket was mine, but it didn't bother me, suddenly I was removed from the light filled tunnel. There wasn't a swooshing sound or feeling of being sucked back into my body, but my environment changed both visually and tactically. The bright light was replaced with intense, but clear blackness. It wasn't foggy or cloud like. It was just a clear darkness. (How can that be more of an oxymoron?)

All the soft, unshaped globs were gone. Now anchored to a base were hard, black, highly polished orbs and obelisks. The glow of light was replaced with intense beams of light. The flashes of light could be likened to a laser show before a rock concert. Sharp beams of narrowly focused light glinted off the surfaces of what appeared to be highly polished granite like substance. The lights were flashing everywhere.

It wasn't scary. It wasn't dreadful. It was just completely different than where I had been before.

And then I felt myself being rushed off the helicopter and through the sunshine of the morning into the emergency room.

I was back. For better or worse, I was back.

Before I was to get better, there was going to be a whole lot of worse.

There was pain. Lots of it. My teeth chattered; the pain was so intense. Triage followed. I hurt so bad I couldn't pray anymore. The room darkened, dimmed. Voices were there. The first I recognized were those of Judy Buckler and Connie Agan – our forever Columbia friends. These sisters had worked with us for all 13 years I had the business in Columbia. Jennifer's frantic call to them interrupted their mall walking. She had already notified the Chamois family and headed west to KU when Barbie intercepted her and told her of the diversion. Not wanting me to be alone, Jennifer instinctively thought of Judy and Connie and called them as she did a U-turn and headed back herself.

My parents and the Starkes arrived together. A pall of deja vu blanketed them. I was delivered to the same ICU where Micah had been pronounced dead. Haven't we just been through this? They dreaded a similar outcome. I don't recall their voices.

The only one I longed for finally came.

"Mike, it's Barbie. I'm here," she said in what was by default my good ear.

When Barbie called the Adrians to ask if they could do car pool on this last day of school, they of course agreed. She explained quickly that she had just received notice that I was being air-lifted to KU's Burn Unit and had to get there ASAP. Ronnie said, "You're not going anywhere that I'm not taking you. I'll be there in five minutes." (Caroline stayed with the Adrians for two weeks until she was allowed to see me.)

As they sped to KU, Barbie roused Justine, by cell phone, from her sleep over at the home of her best friend, Devon Bartel. Knowing how close Justine had been to Cathy, Barbie couldn't bear to tell her the reason I was on the highway to begin with. She only told her of my accident. Justine and Emma-Lea waited for our friends, Jeff and Ann Kranz, to take them to the hospital. Once Barbie called them with the update of the new location, they packed an overnight bag for her and the Kranzes picked them up. Other friends, Fran Cashion and Ginnie Bono, likewise made the same decision. The caravans to Columbia had started.

Rosaries were prayed and many calls exchanged as they fought their way down the closed interstate. The local radio broadcasts continued breaking it with updates. "A state trooper killed in fiery crash. Local businessman fighting for his life." The typically two-hour trip took four due to the traffic, still heavily congested by the clean-up of the wreck.

Barbie knew when she called the ER and was transferred to a social worker instead of a nurse that things were bad. That is exactly what happened when Micah was killed. Social workers talked to us.

She was relieved to hear of no broken bones. That's a good thing. There were burns though, mostly third degree. Some fourth. That's bad. They were very, very deep. That's very, very bad.

Ronnie had barely stopped the car when Barbie started running to the Burn Unit ICU. She again knew the back way. She was the last to arrive to the gathering crowd, some of which had seen me already. Upon seeing Barbie, many started to cry as they hugged her. It was disconcerting. She took one look at my parents and knew what they were thinking. She had to stay composed for them. She entered the cubicle where I lay semi-conscious.

I recall seeing the Wedgwood blue of her blouse out of the slit of my right eye. I never saw her face; she was too close. (I've asked her to never discard that blouse.)

"Dr. Terry had been holding off the debridement procedure until I came, knowing that once they put Mike under, he wouldn't be conscious for awhile. The flesh was just falling off his legs. I couldn't bear to look. His head had absolutely no hair. It was either burned off or the little remaining was shaved off. He smelled like a smoldering log and was very swollen. There was blood draining out of what had been his left ear. I was grateful that Dr. Terry let me be with him privately for a few minutes before they started the cutting," Barbie recalled in her deposition.

"Debridement" is the term used to describe the tearing of dead flesh from the skeleton. Burned flesh will not regenerate. It must be cut away and new tissue transplanted onto the wounds. It is a long, horrific, and painful process. Unfortunately, it's not a one-time procedure either. Though her 20 years as a cardiology nurse helped and her 13 years spent in this very hospital helped, nothing prepared even Barbie Nolte R.N. for the sight of her husband looking like this.

As she ran her hand over my scorched head, she felt a sharp object. A piece of plastic from the car had melted itself onto the back of my skull and, with all the other injuries, had never been noticed. She snapped it off and handed it to the nurses.

Since I had been rolled into the hospital, I inquired again and again, "What about the trooper? What about the trooper?"

No one answered me. They acted as if the question was never asked. Finally I knew I could get the truth. I asked Barbie. (They had been waiting for her to be the one to tell me anyway.)

I whispered to her as she bent down over my head, "Honey, how is the trooper?"

She replied softly, compassionately, "Mike, he didn't make it. He's dead."

I started to cry. Tears streamed out of my right eye. That young boy. His hat larger than his head. Dead. His last words were of compassion.

I told Barbie, "We have to send flowers to his funeral. Can you find out the arrangements from the patrol?" She never answered. She never had time. There were hundreds of flowers there anyway.

My comfort to the Newtons would be almost three years in coming. I was hopeful it would bring more solace than any floral arrangement could, after all, I was the last person on earth with their son and husband. I knew the circumstances in which he died.

By day's end, the waiting room was filled to capacity with friends from everywhere we had lived – Kansas City, Boonville, Chamois, and Columbia. Justine and Emma-Lea were allowed to see me briefly after I had been bandaged. They were overwhelmed by the crowds, the trauma, the look on the faces they knew so well. Justine resisted the urge to throw up and Emma-Lea said every time the elevator opened, more worried friends came rushing out. More friends that separated the girls from a mother that they needed badly at that point.

Barbie is a pragmatic thinker. She knew if she folded, the entire camp of tents would collapse. She felt she was setting an example of positive hope by stating that no one was spending all night at the hospital. That was only necessary when the patient was on the brink of death – her quickly developed opinion of the moment.

"Dr. Terry told me Mike wasn't going to die that night. That's all I needed to hear. We would take the next steps tomorrow. If we let the grief suffocate us, we couldn't help him. It was hard, but I requested that everybody go home," Barbie recalls.

Before they left, friends were allowed in to say their good-byes. By now I was bandaged like a mummy. My legs were wrapped from mid thigh to my toes. My left hand wrapped from fingertips to elbow. My head was encased in gauze with a stretchy net holding it all in place. A central line in my neck went directly into an artery and other IVs into my right hand. There was a small hole cut in the netting for breathing and speaking. Everyone in the cubicle had to be in gowns, gloves, and masks. The risk of infection to a burn victim is his greatest threat. No one could touch me.

"Mike, we're here for you."

"Mike, you're going to make it."

"Mike, don't worry about the girls; just concentrate on pulling through this."

"Mike, everyone we know is praying for you."

The one couple I couldn't say good-bye to though, was Charlene and Jonathan. They had received a cryptic message at the funeral home (that indeed I had asked to have delivered before they loaded me). I had asked a faceless person helping with the stretcher to get the number for Arnold's in Mexico and to call there. I asked them to tell Charlene that I was "going to be a little late" and to start planning without me.

Charlene heard the message. Heard the radio news. Put two and two together and called the hospital from which she had just left the evening before with her sister's body. She brought the first of many care packages with her as she and Jonathan drove the hour to Columbia. Wasn't the worst just behind them?

How can this be happening? To lose Cathy one day and now Mike the next? It was almost a load heavier than they could carry.

My "to-do list" though, was incomplete until Charlene and I had had a catch-up conversation about the plans she had made. I could still give her suggestions for the flowers. Stargazer lilies. The fragrance of which was so delicious that they kept Cathy from attending her mother's wake. Now she was allergy free and could enjoy them.

Before they left, I made Barbie promise that regardless of what was happening to me, she would represent our family by attending Cathy's funeral. She and Emma-Lea did. They brought up the Offertory Gifts for the Requiem Mass the following Tuesday. Obviously I didn't get to deliver the eulogy or be a pallbearer like Cathy had requested. As of this writing, I have yet to visit her grave. I've never seen her tombstone. She will be dead forever. The catalyst of that loss started a life-changing sequence of events for me. I can't bear to really go there yet. Of all the people I have known, she was one of the people who lived her life the closest to God's desires.

Once I was reassured that Cathy was taken care of, there was another group of people I needed to tend to – my brides.

Barbie patiently stood next to my bed stretching the phone to my good ear as I spoke to my staff about the details of the upcoming weddings. There was so much of it in my head and I had left my office a mess the evening before. I knew Stacy would be particularly upset as she and I had become close and she was the last bride with whom I visited. Her files were all over the floor awaiting my return for organization.

I reminded them, "We are using the chair covers twice in one day. First at the Fairmont, then they need to be transferred to Deer Creek Country Club. We are changing the sash colors. Also remember to use caution when delivering Kim Corrigan's Priscilla of Boston gown. The pipe where we usually hang gowns in that church has developed some condensation. In the off chance that it's not fixed yet, and the moisture is rusty, don't take the plastic bag off the shoulders of the gown. And in case I'm not back for the two weddings next week, they've re-carpeted the church where the Cason wedding is happening. The color is more orange red than burgundy red. I've only seen the swatch. Go look at it in person. If the red roses I've ordered don't blend, switch to white. I don't want that to clash in the photographs, and here's a couple of additional things to know... Are you making notes?"

And on and on I talked. Nearly an hour. Never a break. Pure adrenalin. Surprisingly completely lucid. Witnesses to that exchange still can't believe it.

As Barbie's arm and back ached from the arching, she was relieved when the nurse came in and said without asking if I was nearly done, "Enough!"

And she took the phone from Barbie and hung it up.

I couldn't see, but could sense the growing frustration the nursing staff was already experiencing with me. Barbie tried to explain, "He's just this way. He's always been very Type A."

Type A? Hell! I had a business that needed me. I had clients that were depending on me. If I died, there would be an irreplaceable disruption in their wedding plans. Or so I thought.

As the clock neared midnight, the ICU quieted.

The owner of nearby Missouri Manor, a bed and breakfast, had come to the hospital earlier and pressed a note in Barbie's hand insisting that my family come for, "A shower, a nap, an over night...for as long as you need." Little did any of them know it would be 50 nights of lodging that Lyria Bartlett provided for this displaced family. My parents and two daughters had found their way there and Barbie promised to follow.

I needed her to myself.

She needed me to herself.

We needed some time alone.

I asked the nurses to give us some privacy and to slide the glass door closed.

A calm found me.

However, my pain was so intense that I couldn't even place it. All of me was on fire at the same time. I had not seen my body all day, and now my eyes were bandaged shut. I had no idea what damage there had been. I no idea of what was ahead of me. I just knew that right now, I was finally alone with the one who mattered most in the world.

Barbie is the queen of "play down." She always plays things down. Nothing is ever THAT serious. If you told her of an uncle about to have triple bypass, she would dismiss it with news of the latest drugs to prevent future blockages and tell of two patients that she knew who mowed grass three weeks after surgery. Other than Micah's death, I've never heard her say anything is a "big deal."

It was time to get the truth – the truth for which I was completely unprepared.

By now my throat was raspy from the forced talking. The forced cheerfulness to calm the others. I was suddenly exhausted. She explained that they were going to put me to sleep after she left and I would be operated on in the morning. I probably wouldn't wake up before they took me to the O.R. I might not wake up at all tomorrow.

"Barbie, I need to know. Is what has happened to me a 'big deal'?"

Pause.

She leaned close to my ear and squeezed my right hand with her gloved one.

"Mike you've been in a horrible wreck. You've been terribly burned. But they are doing everything they can for you. You're in the best place."

She paused, as her voice choked with emotion.

"Yes...what has happened to you...is a very big deal."

I wasn't frightened. Actually reassured.

I analyzed the situation:

- I was no longer lying on the side of the highway in a field of fescue.
- I had survived the trip to wherever I am and all my family is here.
- There are doctors trying to save my life.
- But if that's not to be, then all that could be done has been done and at 48, my time is up.
- This could be my exit. And I was with the person who I loved most in the world.
- How could it get any better?

She kissed me goodbye and left the ICU in tears.

I didn't wake up for the next 13 days.

FOUR
Too Much Hell

MJN "Too much heaven" BKZ

It's the little things that caused me worry.

The big picture was so out of my control that I knew to not even ask how it was going.

Despite massive drugging while in the ER, I still felt the pressure and pulling, as a nurse used enough torque to cut my wedding band off my left hand.

I worried if I would ever get it back. Was it ruined? Where could I get it replaced?

It is a wide 18-karat gold band – unique in the design of four rows of tiny facets that highlight its surface. When brand new, people often thought it was pavé diamonds it was so sparkling. I've never been into diamonds on guys. I'm glad it wasn't.

Barbie and I had found it at Helzberg's Jewelry in 1980, the year we were married. We both loved it immediately. I didn't try on any others.

Inside she had the jeweler engrave our initials and the title of "our song." The Bee Gee's were riding the wave of another hit when we enjoyed our first date, December 2,1978. After dinner at what was considered Columbia's nicest restaurant, Bobby Buford's, we danced in the lounge. Disco was the rage. The pulsing lights of the dance floor reflected the instant infatuation we felt for each other. We "knew" that night but didn't tell anyone. We were together the next night and the next. After the third date, we told our respective parents, "I've found the person I'm going to marry."

We continued to date every night for three consecutive weeks. Only Christmas Eve split us up as we went to be with our families for the holidays.

On December 26, I put down a deposit on an engagement ring.

The song, "Too Much Heaven," we danced to on our first date always seemed to sum up our relationship.

It was too much heaven.

I was still surprised though when I pulled my ring off on our wedding night (I couldn't sleep with it on for several weeks) and looked inside. There it was, engraved in gold:

Michael Joseph Nolte (in) "Too much heaven" (with) Barbie Kathryn Zeller.

Once I got used to it, the ring seldom came off.

When Trooper Mike Newton asked for my license, I turned to hand it to him with my left hand. That motion caused me to angle my shoulders toward him as well, thus twisting my head to the left.

When the blast of the fireball hit us, all the skin on my ring hand and left side of my head was seared completely off instantly. (Oddly, the long-sleeved shirt I was wearing provided just enough deflection to protect my forearm. My scarring starts exactly where my cuff stopped.)

Now my wedding ring was being cut off, as my body valiantly tried to preserve vital fluids by swelling up. My left hand was badly damaged. Third degree burning goes deep.

Unknowingly, the nurse cut right through the word "heaven." How prophetic? Again, it summed it up. We lost our "heaven" and now we were left to endure the "too much."

And we already thought we had all we could stand these last 11 months with the losses of Micah and Cathy.

The ring was put in a pill bottle and I didn't see it until long after I was home. It was an emotional trigger holding the broken symbol of our commitment. Had the stress equally damaged our marriage? Could the relationship, sometimes at the point of splitting, be re-welded? The symbolism was intense. Yet the ring was not cut in half, only the ends were no longer touching. When could we touch, both figuratively and literally, again?

The first of my eight surgeries started at 6:50 a.m., the morning after the wreck, and lasted five hours and 22 minutes. Barbie was right. I didn't wake up before they wheeled me into operating room, but all my family was standing in the hall praying for Dr. Boyd Terry and his team of burn specialists.

The previous day the surgical team had spent three hours cutting away the charred flesh on my hand, face, toes, feet, legs and thighs. Once past the blackened skin, the dead tissue looks like frostbite, pasty white. All of it had to be manually cut away with scalpels and pliers.

Every successive surgery was an attempt to seal my body; to eventually form its own coating to stave off infection. Round one was to now cover my open wounds with donor skin. Cadaver tissue it is called. This was the very donation that I had discouraged Sherry from allowing. Now in an odd twist, I was the one dependent on the gift made by the family of a loved one who went before me. The tissue bank has such sheets of skin, about the size of a saltine cracker, in reserve for burn victims. That impact will never be lost on me.

These homografts are a vital part to the body's healing, as they trick the body into accepting new patches of skin over the wounds. But homograft transplants will ultimately fail. The permanent skin grafts are those harvested from the patient. They are called autografts.

It takes a very skilled burn doctor to know exactly when to switch the homografts for autografts, and I had the best.

Dr. Terry had already passed retirement but wouldn't give up his burn patients until he had hand-selected his successor. The process to do so had been going on for three years. Temporary fill-ins and probationary doctors came and went. In three-month stints, they were given the chance to carry the torch for burn victims (pun intended) lucky enough to be admitted at University of Missouri Hospital and Clinic. Fortunately for me, Dr. Terry himself was available when Michael Nolte flew in. Without a doubt, he saved my legs.

Dr. Terry and Barbie were a perfect match, though very different personalities. They respected each other tremendously. She didn't ask for much and yet he spoke volumes, using very few words. He made no promises. She made no demands. Each time she was there in her gown, mask, and gloves to help with the dressing changes. Since Barbie was a nurse, the team not only allowed but also appreciated, the extra set of hands as they took down the dressings every other day. Dr. Terry would enter the room when that process was done, quietly, with little, if any, advance notice. His white hair always combed. His bowtie, dapper and crisp. At 68, I saw him in "the unit," as it was known, a minimum of six days a week.

The treatment of burn victims is one of the most specialized fields of intensive care. Most of Barbie's nursing friends related how they tried a rotation in burn care and fainted, threw up, cried with the patients, or had nightmares after hearing them scream in pain. For the burn victim, medical experts say it's the most pain the human body can endure.

Barbie's high school classmate Mary Ellen Winn Gaul walked with her at nursing school graduation. Mary Ellen was a bridesmaid for Barbie. Mary Ellen lived in Kansas City and had worked several years in the burn unit at K.U. Of the few people that could bring Barbie peace, Mary Ellen was the one.

Beating breast cancer and raising two children, Mary Ellen had stepped away from full-time burn care nursing when she saw on the news that I was the survivor. She quickly called her former boss to get answers to Barbie's possible questions before she came to Columbia. She reassured Barbie that Dr. Terry's reputation was stellar nationwide and there was no better care to be received by flying me to another one of the country's 27 burn centers.

She also warned Barbie of the long, long journey that was ahead for me. And that it was going to hurt badly. For a very long time.

I don't think there was enough medicine in the pharmacy to deaden the pain. I was on an IV morphine constant drip, as well as swallowing it orally. When I suffered what is called "break-through pain" (likened to fighting a forest fire) I received bolus (extra) injections into my wrist. In addition I was given Fentynal, Versaid, Ativan, and Ketamine. None of it seemed to help.

After the first surgery I was flooded with enough drugs to create a quasi-coma. Though the nursing staff would work on me, I registered and recalled absolutely nothing for almost two weeks. I was being nourished by a Naso Gastric (NG) tube (in my nose) that fed me 6,000 calories a day. My urine was collected via a Foley catheter that was a part of me for 40 days. Bowel movements were very few, as constipation is a side effect of opiate painkillers.

I just lay there, swollen, bandaged, and unaware of my surroundings, day after day. There was no difference between day and night. Though motionless (and yet sometimes manic) in reality, there was horrible activity in my mind. And of all the parts of the journey that I dread re-living the most to write this book, it would be what I am about to tell you – the hallucinations.

In my estimation, the worst period of our world history was the extermination of the Jews during World War II. What little I knew about it from history class was brought to life with movies like *Sophie's Choice* and *Winds of War*. I had nightmares after both movies and never could bring myself to see *Schindler's List*. I didn't care that it was a story that should be told. I didn't care how many Oscars it won. I absolutely couldn't stand the images of that brutality of one human against another. The thought of touring the death camps as a vacation destination makes me retch. My daughters have taken classes titled, "Holocaust Studies" and read *The Diary of Anne Frank* and *Night*. I simply cannot talk about it or listen to them discuss it. I have no idea what made such an impression on me, but it is the worst form of hell I can imagine, and it was exactly where I lived for nearly two weeks.

In my nightmares I was thought to be a Jew. I knew I was a Catholic, but the Nazis wouldn't believe me. As a result, my family suffered just like the Jews. We weren't, however, in the 1940s. It was the present day. The Nazis had invaded the United States. We were captured and separated. I knew Barbie and the girls were not together as I could yell to her in another building where they were beating her. I could hear her screaming and between beatings, she would yell back to me what she knew of the girls.

Our daughters had been taken together to a barn where they were being raped, over and over by Nazi soldiers. From where Barbie was imprisoned, she could hear the girls. None of us could see each other and I was constantly trying to escape to save my family. In my mind, I was not injured, but rather healthy and a specimen for the experiments that Josef Mendel would perform on living humans until he killed them. I could hide behind doors, under beds, and above the ceiling tiles, but they would always find me. Just as I thought it was safe, I would be apprehended and punished.

(I wonder now if those "soldiers" weren't indeed my nurses who did, in fact, inflict horrific pain during the course of their job.)

In reality the mini-blinds of my room opened not to a lawn but to the roof of another building. That building had two pipes protruding several feet into the air. White smoke came out of them most of the time.

In my hallucinogenic mind, the blinds became the bars of my cell or the barbed wire of my pen. The steaming pipes were the chimneys of the crematoriums where they would destroy the bodies of the Jews after killing them in the gas chambers. Some of the Jews weren't completely dead when they started to burn them.

I was one of those Jews. I knew that they were about to burn me alive. The sight of the steaming pipes caused me to throw up (in reality) and be the most frightened I have ever been in my life. I couldn't tell Barbie any of this though, as I didn't want her to worry. I wanted her to think I was always coming to save her and together we would rescue our daughters.

The nightmares never, never ended.

I have studied my medical charts to determine which exact drug caused this horrific side effect and in essence, it could have been any number of them or the combination of them. Under no circumstance in the future would I want to be put that far down with opium-based drugs. I would rather have the pain, and the pain was the worst I've ever experienced.

Barbie realized from my sweating and moaning that I was suffering and correctly guessed that it was more mental than physical. She was worried about a brain injury and requested a psychiatric consultant be brought in. Dr. Terry assured her that this behavior was not unexpected, as my injuries were so severe it was my mind's way of not registering pain.

Into the second week of this, though, she received a visit from her former cardiology boss, Dr. Greg Flaker. She shared her concern for my mental state and asked if he thought a different medicine would make a difference in my anguish and gibberish. He suggested Haldol. Barbie was shocked. That was, using her term, – a big dog drug – and used only when necessary to completely knock out a patient after open heart surgery. This was for people who were very, very sick.

Ativan was exchanged for Haldol. Maybe because of that, maybe not, I calmed.

Eventually they could start bringing me back "up" again.

I was propped up in a recliner beside my bed when I "came to" in the afternoon of June 5. The nurse that was to become my favorite, Kandra

Voshage, was working on the bandages on my feet. She and her husband Merit were going to Kansas City for a Pearl Jam concert. She was asking Barbie for a downtown hotel recommendation. I stepped right into that conversation and said, "The Marriott on 12th Street. I'll call my friend Joyce Spencer there and make the reservation for you."

Everyone in the room just stopped. Tears filled my mom's eyes.

Barbie said, "Welcome back, sleepy head."

Kandra looked up and remarked, "Looks like I see some lights on in there."

I was serious about the hotel reservation and insisted on getting the phone call placed. As Kandra objected, Mom insisted, "Let him do it. He has to do it."

And I did.

I don't know who was more surprised, Joyce Spencer, or the people in the room listening to my end of the conversation. Joyce kindly provided the room complimentary to Kandra as a "thank you" for the fine nursing she was doing for me.

And from then on, I was "fully present."

Being "present" though was not always a blessing.

The second equally horrible part of the burn recovery, that no one can possibly imagine, is the process of debridement. The first time it was done with scalpels and pliers the afternoon of the wreck it took three hours.

For the remainder of my weeks in the ICU, I endured debridement every other day. It is essentially the removal of all skin that has been deemed necrotic or dead. Some of this is tissue that died after the initial resection. Some of it was skin grafts that didn't take or had failed. Now the flesh and scabs were pulled off with big tweezers.

Every burn victim I've encountered dreads the process. It is performed in a torture chamber known as the Hubbard Tank. Thus it is referred to as going "to the tank."

Some tanks are large whirlpools and the patient is lowered in lying in a basket. Mine was a shower chair.

The debridement was administered in a windowless room down the hall from the Burn Unit. The room itself was about 8'x8'. Just big enough for the tank itself, a wheelchair, Dr. Terry, two nurses and a naked patient.

Add to that cast, in my case, a photographer.

The lawyers required as evidence for the lawsuit, photographs of my treatment. If the pain hadn't been so bad, I would have been embarrassed but Kent, the photographer, was very sensitive and skillful as to how he angled his lens.

The tank was essentially a stainless bench sitting in a wading pool. Sterile towels formed a non-slippery base for my seat and footrest. Sterile sheets of plastic covered all the metal parts. Jointed flute-style tubes of steel squirted water over my body, starting at the shoulders. The tubes could be positioned like lobster claws to spray away the blood and pus that was constantly being washed into the pool below.

Getting out of the wheelchair, nude and onto the seat, was always the worst part. I couldn't bear any weight, as the soles of my feet were burned off and both Achilles tendons burned as well. Every toe had been burned top and bottom, as they sat motionless in puddles of flaming gasoline. A suspected air draft on the right side of the car burned that area even hotter. Like a welder's torch, the fire burned through the bone in my right leg.

Standing to pivot was excruciating. I nearly passed out each time I had to do it.

Once on the seat, the nurses would monitor my breathing and blood pressure. As soon as the layers of bandages were saturated, they would start unwrapping them from my limbs. With each last layer would come loose tissue. Imagine pulling off a band-aid from a wound that went from the tip of your toes to the middle of your thighs every other day!

I sat often with my eyes closed so I didn't have to watch my body bleed. I would take shallow breaths when they would warn me, "You're going to feel a little tug." Ice chips placed in my mouth allowed me to focus on the cold and kept me from vomiting into the pool.

There was never any conversation in the room. Everyone knew how badly this hurt and they hurried as fast as they could. I found relief in hearing "all done" in regard to the area they were working on: ear, face, neck, hand, left thigh, right thigh, left leg, right leg, left foot, right foot. I called out my pain levels periodically as a cue for more painkiller to be injected. It was never lower than an 8.

I would survive my time in the tank by the ticking of the sweep hand on the clock in front of me. The process took two hours.

I would break two hours down into eight quarters and those quarters into four sets of 15 minutes each.

Furthermore, I would then sub-divide the segments of 15 minutes into three sets of five minutes.

Those five minutes got sub-sub-divided into individual minutes.

Those minutes were sub-sub-sub-divided into 60... sweeping... seconds... each.

I knew I could not bear the pain a full two hours, but maybe I could bear it for just another minute...which when multiplied by five...became a third of a quarter...of an hour...

And if I could just string together four of those sets of "quarter of an hour(s)."

I would have the debridement half finished.

For that day.

It took everything I had to just keep breathing through debridement. I wanted them to stop! I just wanted to stop – stop feeling, stop living, stop existing.

It was during that time that I experienced the closest moments I've ever known with Christ.

Finally it was over. The water turned off. New bandages applied. I was lifted back into my wheelchair and rolled back into my room where a freshly changed bed awaited me. I was home!

I was back in the intensive care burn unit! And I was glad for it?! That's how bad it was.

I would lay there trembling and so thankful to have it over. Now I could look forward to tomorrow, another day in the ICU, but a day I referred to as "having off." No debridement.

People who have never been through the process have no idea what a burn victim goes through.

It was truly too much.

FIVE
The Burn Unit Fish Bowl

On May 22 and 23, the headline of every Missouri newspaper and lead news story of every television station was news of the wreck. More specifically, the preventable death of a state trooper killed in the line of duty.

For the Kansas City stations and the Kansas City Star, much of their coverage focused on the survivor: "Area business owner fighting for his life," "Support pours out for local leader," "Friends shocked at tragedy for a family that stepped out of a Norman Rockwell drawing," all either headlines or verbiage used by the news teams.

Crews were dispatched to the crash site and then to make the five o'clock news, to my store and my home. Using both as background, they conducted interviews with brides, employees, and neighbors. Crash victims don't typically get air lifted 100 miles from home, and thus the imagined horror was magnified to most. Many people have told me that they remember exactly where they were when they heard the news.

The support for my family came like an avalanche. The Kansas City friends came in car pools and the Columbia friends came frequently. Seldom was the waiting room not used as a receiving room for Barbie to accept the gifts of flowers, fruit, and candy that people brought with them. As the cards started arriving, my daughters taped them to the walls. Eventually the walls were covered ceiling to floor, edge to edge, all four walls.

Mail call was a welcome respite to the day. When the girls were visiting, I would open the card, show it to them and read the entire verse aloud to them before revealing the sender's identity. (Like I had seen their elementary teachers do with reading books to the class.) They made a game out of it. If they didn't know the sender, the explanation of our relationship was a pleasant remembering. It was a good shared time. The cards lifted my spirits every day. I couldn't accept flowers in ICU and remember regretfully receiving a two-level cart full one day. The volunteer pushed it to the glass door of my room and Emma-Lea read all the cards to me. I gave the arrangements to my three shifts of nurses that day to take home.

I was taught how to be a friend by my friends during those weeks. I received cards from people that I had thought forgotten, but they had some loose connection to us through a mutual friend. The cards particularly from former newlyweds really touched me. These were couples (or their parents) that I had often kept at a professional distance. I justified it by thinking the emotional detachment would keep me more efficient the day they needed me to have the only level head.)

I don't know whom I was kidding. I'm a hugger, both in words and gesture. But to sense that closeness returned was very affirming.

People would write the most encouraging memories of our times together, 15 to 20 years ago. They had added me to their church's prayer chains all over the country. Almost 600 of the cards were from former brides.

I also received cards from strangers. People up and down I-70 had read the story. Perhaps they knew a burn victim, knew a trooper or were self-employed. Whatever the connection, they reached out to me. I will never forget it. The letters continued for months and still there are notes of encouragement that follow every speaking engagement.

My friend Cindy Bartel, (Devon's mother), created a video of well wishes from the guys in my Men's Group, co-retailers in the community, and my neighbors on the cul-de-sac. She filmed my house, now with thick green grass and the roses blooming like they do each June (whether I'm home or not).

Arranged on my driveway was an arch of lawn chairs. My neighbor Bill McVay, "toasted" me (on camera) with a cold one in hand and pointed to the chair that was empty and waiting for me to come home.

I did have a home! I did have a life before being burned! (Would it be too unrealistic to think that maybe some day I can go back there?) I watched the video over and over.

My glasses, destroyed in the wreck, were replaced, but still I couldn't concentrate to read and television just added to my anxiety level. Likewise, visitors were not a welcome distraction and with rare exception, I did not feel up to company. Barbie had to beg me to receive visitors. She pointed out that some had driven a long way or returned for several days. Allowing them to see me wasn't for me but rather what they needed. Sometimes they would just come in and cry; maybe because of how bad I looked or maybe because of how relieved they were that I looked that good. I've decided that visitors to a patient in ICU are, for the most part, always stress inducing for the patient.

Even short phone calls would cause me to break into a sweat as I labored to just think of how to develop the next line of conversation. Eventually I asked to have the phone unplugged. I just couldn't take it. My room was filtered with purified air to lower the risk of infection. The on and off of the blower made me nuts. I asked if they could just leave it permanently turned on. I just craved quiet and tranquility. I could barely concentrate because of the pain. Every stimulus provoked anxiety.

Sweating was a big part of my experience as my body's thermostat had been ruined and I alternated between soaking the sheets and freezing. I sustained a fever for weeks.

In the early days, I was too weak to feed myself and my sisters would cut up the hospital Jell-o and feed it to me. The IV tubes kept knocking things off my lunch tray as I would try to reach for something. Once I figured out how to guard the IVs in the back of my hand, I could navigate a lunch tray. I had the nervous habit of constantly drinking huge pitchers of ice water and in reality that was a very good thing. I sweat so much that the water countered dehydration and the fluids were important for new skin regeneration. But the urine collection bags – those lovely urine collection bags – had to be frequently emptied. Not just discreetly emptied, but held up the light, poured into a measuring device, output recorded, and then re-attached to my Foley.

I learned how our body wants to heal itself. Luckily I went into this life-threatening condition being a non-smoker, not overweight, not a diabetic, and with normal blood pressure. Any of those factors would have severely hampered my recovery.

I learned that my circulatory system had been greatly impaired as so many veins had been burned away or destroyed in debridement. As new ones were being formed, the blood supply went to help the most wounded body parts first – my extremities of feet, hands, and face. Thus when I finished a meal, the digestive system needed blood to break down the food's nutrients. I pictured an "all call" going out to the edges of my body. Like troops, the blood came running back into the center of the camp (my abdomen) and leaving the rest of me shivering.

I developed my own mini-furnace for this predictable daily occurrence and asked if a blow dryer could be attached to my headboard. After supper, I would elevate the bottom of the bed and create a tent with my sheets. I would aim the blow dryer inside, trapping the warm air over my torso. The night shift could hear the blow dryer running at all hours of the night if I awakened and had forced some more food down.

In spite of the 6,000 calories going through my nose every day and the nasty tasting protein shakes I had to drink, I still melted away. In its Herculean effort to heal itself, the body needs lots of fuel. Calories are fuel. Food contains calories. My healing was so intense that there wasn't enough "coal in the furnace." All my fat was being used for fuel. The hospital dietician begged me to eat all I possibly could.

When I finally was able to balance on a scale, I was shocked to see that I had lost 30 pounds in a month. Now the term "concentration camp victim" really had personal meaning to me. I couldn't believe it. "Gaunt" would be a polite adjective to describe my appearance.

Being a long-term patient in ICU is akin to living in the proverbial fish bowl. One entire wall was glass, and it was preferred that the drapery remain open. I was in "Bed 1," next to the back hallway doors that automatically opened to allow a new admission in or to roll a patient out. If the top of the stretcher was flat and the sheet almost touched the floor, Barbie had explained that a corpse was on a shelf below the top of the gurney and was being taken to the morgue.

Such was the case with others while I was in-house.

Mr. Swan, 84, had burned his back when his pajamas caught fire in his attempt to fry bacon on a gas range. He suffered from dementia as well and didn't call for help for three days. His daughter found him lying on the kitchen floor wrapped in a throw rug. The nurses would patiently walk him around the unit and I would see him shuffle by my door. He yelled in pain throughout the night. One day he suffered a heart attack and his pain was over. They rolled him past my door under a flat sheet.

Tara, a 20-year-old new mother from Oklahoma, contracted a flesh eating bacterial infection from her episiotomy during delivery of her child. Her six-week-old daughter was in the waiting room with her 19-year-old, tattooed father and religious conservative maternal grandparents. She had been in three hospitals before they heard of the work Dr. Terry could do with tissue transplants. She was on a vent the entire time she was in our unit. My parents became close to this woman's parents and often cared for the baby so the grandparents could be at their daughter's bedside. She was rolled past my door under a flat sheet.

The Fourth of July was a busy day for admissions to the Burn Unit. Extra staffing was in place for the predictable fireworks-related injuries. Rolling past my door that evening was a 15-year-old boy who had swallowed a bottle rocket. He and two friends had watched a show called "Jack-ass" where stupid tricks were staged. Hoping to get on the show, they armed themselves with a video recorder, helmets, and fireworks. As one friend served as cameraman, the other lit the bottle rockets and aimed them toward the third. This last non-Mensa candidate, protected his head with a helmet and hoped to catch the bottle rocket with his teeth. The first one missed. The second one was on target. The kid lost a chunk of his mouth and burned off his lips.

There were also the frequent "in and outs" of those dummies who thought that "just a little gas" would help jump-start their pile of smoldering brush. The smolder ignited the stream of gas back up to the can, to the hand holding it, to the arm, attached to the hand.

And then there were the lawbreakers – the meth operators. Frequently that was the hushed qualification for their right to get free treatment in this state-funded burn unit. They had blown themselves up in a meth lab! Theirs were the families that usually took over the waiting room, sleeping on sofas all day, starting fights and knocking over lamps, playing a boom box while others tried to watch television. These families were indignant when they were denied access to their patient...right now! They didn't care about a posted visitor's schedule. Those rules were for others. They were entitled to have the exception made. (Barbie told me, "As bad as it is for you in here, you're in a better place than we are in that waiting room today.")

I was amazed to learn that some of these same "victims" would argue with the physical therapist when she wouldn't write a prescription authorizing their Medicaid to pay for a wheelchair for them. She assessed they didn't need it and she wasn't going to enable them. Their burns were often minor. It was incredulous to me to think anyone would want to settle for less than the fullest rehabilitation they could manage.

Physical therapy and occupational therapy for me were always an experience of movement, literally of course, but also figuratively. I was finally moving toward a goal – the goal of going home! But that ultimate goal came with many mini-goals to be accomplished first.

After lying on my back for so many weeks with my legs in sheepskin-lined plastic splints, I couldn't imagine the sensation of being vertical again.

The latest skin grafts had been harvested from my lower abdomen and my quadriceps. I had a reverse Speedo tan line. Typically that V would be the lighter skin due to no exposure to the sun. In my case, that area was the tanner skin as it was left intact (thankfully). The areas below and above where the Speedo would be worn were peeled with an instrument like a cheese slicer, peeling off layers of skin. Now those areas were bloody, oozing, and starting their own healing.

The "harvest sites," as they are known, hurt worse than the graft sites. The intensity of the extreme stinging was made even more uncomfortable as it also felt like an abdominal incision. As the sites healed over with new skin, the itching under the bandages was as bad as the stinging. As soon as the newest crop of skin was solid, just like sod in a field, it was harvested again and the healing process started all over. This surgery took place three times.

After surgery number five or six, I was so discouraged that I finally got the courage to ask Dr. Terry a few direct questions. (Previously, because I didn't want the answers, I never asked many questions.)

"Dr. Terry, will I ever stand again?"

"Yes."

"Will I be able to walk again?"

"Yes."

(And then with no previous thought to this wording:)

"Will I be able to dance with my daughters at their weddings?"

Pause.

"I believe so. But not in the way you would have before your injury."

I'll take that. Faith restored.

I was going to get better. I had a reason to believe it now. Dr. Terry had said it would be so.

The Physical Therapy department was in the hospital's lowest level. It's director, Corie Roth Taylor, had been married the weekend after the wreck and was new to both Columbia and the job. She was, however, a pro. Her assistant, Sue Glasgow, was a 13-year veteran of P.T. The director of the Occupational Therapy department was Cathy Barrow.

This trio of caring individuals worked closely with Kandra and Paul Linneman (Dr. Terry's physician's assistant) in every facet of my care. Together they readied me for the eventual first "stand." As simple as that sounds – to stand up – it was subject to a very rehearsed strategy. By now, the MRI had revealed the source of the extreme amount of pain associated with weight bearing. The bone near my ankle had been burned completely through. Not just to the bone, but *through* the bone. The precious fascia that coats the bone was gone for several inches in several places. The hole in my leg was black and deep. At a dressing change, Dr. Terry pulled back the bandages to the point that he could reach in my leg and wiggled the black bone. Unfortunately Barbie was present and nearly fainted.

He explained that unless life-giving blood could be brought back into that marrow, the leg would have to come off. I asked what would be the advantages of amputation and was told my healing would be faster and less painful. When I learned that he could drill for blood only three times, I prayed he would "strike oil" and he did on the third and final try.

For several days prior, I was to simply dangle my legs (with the help of two morphine tablets) off the bed for as long as I could stand blood rushing into the swollen limbs. On the day I took "the stand," I also received a bolus of morphine in my vein, in addition to the tablets. In five minutes I was ready to accept a helper under each arm for the task.

The staff would raise the bed to a level that allowed me to simply slide off the mattress rather than having to push up with my knees to stand. Knowing the pain that was coming, just getting mentally prepared to do this took almost 20 minutes. The staff's patience and encouragement was unbelievable.

"Come on, Mike. You can do this."

"Just slide your bottom off when you're ready, and we're here to help you."

"You'll be so glad when you've got this behind you."

"I know this is a big step. You've been doing so well with all the little ones so far."

"You only need to stand up 'straight.' Not stand long."

My feet were bandaged and cushioned and protected by plastic coverings that were molded to the new shape of my feet.

Finally, like diving off the high board the first time, I did it! I stood! For only three seconds and then fell back on my bed, soaked in sweat, but I had done it!

And that's how my rehab started. One stand, one step at a time.

The next day, I stood for 10 seconds. Same ending though.

Eventually I was ready for the ride to the P.T. room. I was excited, nervous, flushed, drugged.

As I entered, I was introduced to that department's cheerful staff and had positive anticipation for whatever was about to happen. Then Cathy rolled me around the corner – there in the middle of the room it stood.

"And there's your walker. Just waiting for you."

I lost it. Completely lost it.

I couldn't touch my face, but my chin went to my chest. Sobs racked my body.

How could I have come to this?! A walker? I'm only 48! A walker is for old people who can't walk alone. Or worse than that natural decline, a walker is for the disabled.

I wasn't either.

But wait. Yes I was.

I, Michael J. Nolte, age 48, had to accept the fact that I was disabled.

I couldn't walk without assistance.

I for sure couldn't walk without this device – tennis balls, rolling wheels and a tote bag on the front bar. I needed a walker.

It was a low, low day.

That was all I could take. Not expecting that reaction, but gratefully, not expecting more from me then, Cathy rolled me back up to my room. I cried off and on, most of that evening. Thank you God, no visitors. I just couldn't believe it. (How many, many times would I utter those words to myself?)

The next day I asked to go back to P.T.

This time "the boogey man" of a walker wasn't going to spook me. It was reduced in my mind as simply a means to reach my goal.

The staff wrapped me in double gowns to cover my backside, arranged my IV poles and catheter bag to walk beside me. Today Cathy tried a new approach. I was going to stand up and walk the parallel bars first. Then I would transition to the walker.

At the end of the parallel bars, Sue positioned a full-length mirror so I could check my form while walking. Back straight, butt in. Abdominal incision pain be damned.

The goal was to get myself out of the chair without assistance and take just one step. She demonstrated the sequence.

After three false "Okay, I'm ready" announcements, I pushed up from my wheelchair arms, lunged for the bars and pulled myself upright! I paused to get my balance. The room swirled. My legs screamed in pain. And I stood straight... briefly.

Cheers all around!

Then determined to "Just do it," I took my first tentative step allowing weight on my left foot.

I repositioned my hands and hopped forward another step. Two!

Then I inched forward a bit more and hopped again, this time letting my right foot touch the tile. Three! Three steps!

And then I looked in the mirror.

What I saw looking back was an emaciated, pasty pale, sweaty kid with only stubble for hair, malformed legs, a saggy hospital gown, a bag of pee, some tubes hooked to him and bandages over much of his body.

I looked like someone who was recovering from a catastrophic car wreck.

And I was that person.

I had never seen my reflection until that moment. In 24 hours, the physical therapy experience had taken me from the horizontal plane that I had adapted to as normal, to realizing that I was indeed disabled. It wasn't a prediction or worst fear.

It was a reality. And now I had evidence that I even looked the part.

I've never considered myself handsome in the GQ sense of the word, but I always did the best I could with what I had. I shaved every morning. Showered twice a day. Brushed my teeth after every meal. Went to a hair stylist, used "product," even got highlights. I took care of my clothes and wore socks that matched my pants. Friends gave me grief about so many horses on my shirts. I loved to swim and the tan that came with it. And now this.

Again, a major melt down. My mom and Barbie were there on the sidelines and it was almost too much for them as well. I think seeing me hurting so much emotionally was killing them mentally. There's not much pain relief for that kind of hurt. I just slumped back into the wheelchair and bawled my head off.

I decided that was the last of that kind of breakdown. (Words to eat.) From there on, I progressed rapidly each day. I mastered bouncing on the big rubber ball to develop core strength and balance. I could get into and out of my wheelchair with the help of an over-head pull bar.

If the goal was to walk three steps, I would walk 10.

The next day it was to repeat the 10. I would walk 15.

From 15 to 30.

From 30 to 40.

From 40 to half way around the PT track. As I shuffled with my walker, Sue would follow me pushing my wheelchair and shepherding the poles and tubes attached to me. If I needed to sit quickly, to avoid fainting, she was right there with a cold cloth and ice water.

"Mr. Nolte, Mr. Nolte, I can barely keep up with you. Look at you go."

Every time I had afternoon visitors, they trekked with me to P.T. and served as additional cheerleaders.

Sue gave me the ultimate compliment near the end of my stay when she told me I was only the second patient in her 13 years that said they looked forward to P.T. I couldn't believe it. She said that most patients just give up or give in. PT hurts.

Well hell yes, it hurts. But not like debridement. And I had already survived that.

Hell yes it hurts, but not like having my own skin peeled off my stomach and stapled onto my legs. I had survived that three times!

I wasn't going to come this far and stop now...because of pain.

As I worked to regain my abilities, I also worried about my re-crafted appearance.

Three weeks before the wreck, our family sat for a portrait with my friend Isaac Alongi. He's widely known as the best black and white photographer in Kansas City. The shoot lasted only 20 minutes. What he captured will last a lifetime.

The day of the wreck, he saw the news and had the forethought to quickly produce an 8x10 enlargement and paid one of his employees to drive it to Columbia. Not knowing the damage to my face, he wanted the doctors to have a recent photo for re-construction.

I don't know if it helped Dr. Terry in any way, but we all knew the goal of final healing.

I watched my fingertips deteriorate into E.T.-like charcoal crisp husks. The tendons and ligaments tightened under the newly grafted skin and I couldn't bend my knuckles. As I saw my legs oozing blood and sheets of skin just floating on fluid until it attached by gravity to my muscle, I couldn't imagine ever looking normal again. Then I received a visit from Jimmy.

Six months earlier, in December, he finished cutting firewood with a chainsaw. He took off his flannel shirt, placed the chain saw on the shirt, filled his woodstove with logs and went to sleep. Upon waking, Jimmy noticed the house was cold, so he slipped on the flannel shirt to carry in some logs.

The chain saw had dripped gasoline all night onto his shirt. When he leaned forward to toss in the logs, a spark ignited his sleeves, which transformed him into a torch. He rolled on the floor to extinguish the flames, wrapped himself in a wet rug and drove himself to the hospital. Driving a stick and unable to shift, he tore out his transmission before finally getting to the ER.

Jimmy was having a check-up in the burn clinic down the hall from the unit. He stopped by to visit any of us newbies. His good intentions aside, I blamed Cathy (my O.T.) of sending him to me as reverse psychology. She laughed at the notion, but it worked.

Jimmy's arms and neck were terribly scarred and still Pepto pink. He was wearing a too-small, bright orange t-shirt. When I shook his hand, his fingers didn't bend. It was like shaking a fan blade. He told me to stay encouraged about my outcome and proceeded to show me evidence of the "great job" done on him. He raised his shirt and revealed his belly and chest.

It looked like pink spaghetti had been glued to his body. I was shocked by his candor and amazed at his comfort.

As soon as he left, Cathy stopped by to check on my progress of using the hand rehab squeeze thingy. It was a contraption created of increasing tension by shorter and shorter rubber bands. Its benefit was to restore range of motion in my fingers to the point I could make a fist.

"Stiff" didn't hurt. Bending hurt like hell. Cathy insisted that I squeeze this appliance open and shut several times a day.

I asked her if I was going to end up looking like Jimmy and she said with certainty, "No."

"Why not? How do you know?"

"Because you are already more physician-compliant at this stage than Jimmy has been in five months."

Oh. So whatever that means, makes a difference? (I didn't know I had a vote in how I would end up looking.)

Cathy went on to explain that Jimmy's scarring was so pronounced because he thought the moisturizer smelled too "sissy." There is a special lotion created for burn victims to replace moisture in their healing skin that has no moisture pores. It is to be applied multiple times a day forever. He wouldn't use it.

I had been wearing a Jobst glove on my right hand once the bandages came off. It was custom sized to be slightly smaller than my hand, thus fit very tightly. (My legs would eventually get tights made of the same patented Spandex as well.) These compression garments, as they are called in the burn world, are critical to holding scarring to a minimum. As skin rebuilds itself, it grows wild like an untrained grapevine. It needs to be molded into the desired shape. This constant pressure is painful but essential to flatten out the scarred tissue.

Jimmy found his compression sleeves and vest too itchy and hot. When his electricity was cut off, he had no AC, thus they became even hotter, and he stopped wearing them all together. (I would wear my compression tights for almost two years.)

And finally his fingers were permanently left frozen because using the rubber band appliance...well...it hurt. So it got pitched aside.

If I ever needed additional motivation to not give up or give in, I just got it.

The nervous habit of always sucking down water was now joined by nervously squeezing the hand rehabber constantly. I broke so many rubber bands they just finally brought me my own box full.

How can I write this book with the intent of giving patients, burn victims, and their families a complete picture of what it's like to be confined to the ICU for more than two months?

I've touched on many facets of the journey – surgery, hallucinations, drugs, treatments, pain, rehab therapy, support and hope, physical conditions, and motivation. If I were a male patient rendered helpless, I would wonder/worry about how the personal needs are handled.

When *Tuesdays with Morrie* was a best seller, I read it with interest and remembered the demarcation Morrie made for knowing it couldn't get any worse. As his Lou Gehrig's disease progressed, he slowly lost his abilities. He became a prisoner of his body. Gradually he lost the ability to walk, dress himself, feed himself, clean himself. When he reached the point that somebody had to clean him up after a bowel movement, he was finished.

I started in that condition.

As a healthy, on-top-of-my-game, capable, fast moving, fast thinking, even fast talking, 48-year-old man with a tan, I was rendered completely dependent on others in 1.8 seconds.

I don't recall exactly how many nights it was before the wreck that Barbie and I made love. I know it wasn't the night before, but it would be a whole bunch of nights before we ever did again. And I hurt so badly, I didn't care. (Now, guys, that's a lot of pain!)

To stare at a Foley catheter coming out of your body and thinking about how it got there is enough to make me shudder still. Fortunately I was unconscious when that happened. I wanted to be sure that it didn't get jiggled loose and need to be re-inserted. The advantage was of course that I never needed to call for a urinal or worse than that, need help holding one. I never was awakened because of a full bladder. My female nurses were always very sensitive about allowing me private cleaning time alone during their daily sponge bath ritual. The kidney function piece of this was manageable. Wherever I went, the urine bag followed…gurney, wheelchair, tank, physical therapy, waiting room, O.R. Always there, disgustingly present.

The other bodily function, bowel movements, yes, I've finally said it, bowel movements, were more embarrassing, painful, and challenging. Due to constipation, suppositories were a necessity every three days. It was on the chart if my bowels hadn't moved or if they had. Gross. Fortunately this was an under-the-covers, probe and push action, but even so, I would wait for evening visitors to leave before I started this three-hour labor.

Just like labor increases in intensity before childbirth and delivery, so were the contractions of my lower intestine as its contents were finally expelled. I had never had a suppository in my life. I didn't know what to expect or how long they took to work. It was immediately uncomfortable. As the medicine melted and was absorbed in my digestive tract, I broke into a sweat. The pushing, clenching, gritting caused me to grip the bed rails as I rolled from side to side trying to hurry along the process.

Getting out of bed onto a commode wasn't an option. I couldn't have my legs down. Getting a bedpan under me wasn't an option either, I had too many bandages on my thighs. So with every ounce of normalcy I could muster, I would call the nurse and ask her to bring me a clean hand towel to use as my chamber pot. Once the job was completed, I felt like a puppy that had just soiled the carpet. I was mortified each time.

With one hand completely stitched and bandaged and the other usually the home of the IV needle, I was helpless to clean up myself. It struck me instantly that I was where Morrie most dreaded to be. It truly is the most humiliating of the patient experiences. It was so awful that I couldn't even decide if it was worse or better with a nurse of either gender. But that Burn Unit crew – if ever there was dignity to be given to the most undignified job, they did it.

Looking back, requesting a stool softener would have shortened the process. But I just didn't want to talk about it.

The day the Foley came out was Day 40. For some reason, Dr. Terry decided it had to come out that day. Not the next when I would have the benefit of conscious sedation.

Kandra told of his order.

I told her I wanted to wait a day.

She countered with waiting until after lunch.

I caved and said "I'll dread it until it's done. Let's do it now."

In her usual, "this is typical and no big deal" manner, Kandra gloved her hands, explained that she was going to deflate the balloon in my bladder ("Balloon in my bladder?!) and "on three" extract the tubing. What she didn't say was that the tubing was lodged somewhere near my Adam's apple and would take an eternity to extract.

She gave me a "head's up" (pun intended) by saying: "Now, you'll feel a little pressure."

What I've learned about hospital lingo is "pinch" means "stab," "tug" means "pull your flesh out," and "pressure" means "you won't be able to breathe until I'm done." And that was the case. Pull, pull, pull, pull. I've seen anchors come out off the sea bottom quicker and easier than this garden hose came out of my loins.

Stinging. Stinging. Was there flesh attached to that pipe? It lifted my hips off the sheets. But at least it was out.

That afternoon Jimmy stopped by again. I told him I was less one tube. He caused me to begin sweating when he told me, "You know they only give you four hours to pee on your own. Otherwise they stick it back it in. I had mine stuck back in three times."

I looked at the clock. I had 45 minutes left! I started downing every liquid in sight – ice water, grapefruit juice, left over skim milk, and asked for iced tea to be made...quickly!

Right at the four-hour mark, I felt "the urge" for the first time in 40 days. Thank heaven!

I readied the urinal, (now about to be a permanent fixture on my bedside table.......empty or full........always an unattractive decor accent piece.)

The stream – that's what they call pee in a hospital – started, burned, stopped, started, burned, stopped. Stopped. Stopped.

Kandra came by and echoed what Jimmy had predicted. I indicated my accomplishment and she said that wasn't nearly enough to be considered normal output. I was NOT going in reverse with that Foley. I gulped ice tea for another hour and tried again. Same slow start, very painful burning, which caused the stop. (The body's own check valve for pain I guess.)

I remembered how in the tank, the ice chips helped me concentrate on an alternate sensation. I created my own distraction. I swung my legs off the bed, pointed the heat of the blow dryer at my crotch, and started the stream again.

Between the throbbing in my legs and the heat blast to my groin, I "out-pained" my penis. The battle of the Foley was won.

Excitedly, I called Barbie to report that today, "I walked a little and peed a lot."

SIX
Faith Rocks

"For I know the plans I have for you,
says the Lord. They are plans for good...
to give you a future and a hope."
Jeremiah 29:11

The cards kept rolling in. Thank you God for inventing Hallmark.
I needed every single one.

I never received the acquaintances that tried unceasingly to convince the security desk that they were close friends.

I seldom felt up to even seeing the honest-to-goodness friends that, at great inconvenience, took off work, made the drive, fought the traffic, managed the parking garage and followed the labyrinth of the hospital to eventually get to the Burn Unit, often to hear, "He's just not up to company this afternoon." And I'm a people person!

Those in the "Golden Circle," though, were granted admission, but they had to pass the inquisition of both Mrs. Noltes first.

But the one thing that I always appreciated, was being reminded that there was indeed a world out there and that there were people who were pulling for me. The cards were tangible evidence of that caring. And many people didn't just send one, but several. What a difference a hand written attached note would make. I could read it at rest. I could read in pain. I could read it when I was on the verge of crying. I could feel their arms around me. There were days I needed that.

My friend Christy Huber sent the opening verse on a card.

The Hubers of Omaha hired me nine years earlier to coordinate their only daughter Nikki's glorious wedding. They are very authentic people. We remained friends ever since. Christy is a prayer warrior and a big believer in her prayer being heard constantly when accompanied with the lighting of the large nine-day votive candles in her church. After the wedding, they sent me two crystal (very expensive I think), heart paperweights. One ruby. One amethyst. One from each of them. I treasure them – the   appreciation gift – and the Hubers. It was not a surprise that they sent a card during my darkest hour. It was a surprise that they realized this was a long ordeal and they kept sending cards. I knew that she had read every verse, chosen every cover. Nothing about Christy Huber is not thoughtfully considered first.

The day I received the lavender card with the above scripture quote, I really, really needed to be reminded that He had a plan for me that wasn't just what I was feeling today but rather a future – a good future – and that I should expect soon to feel "hope."

It would be a while.

"My God, my God, why have you forsaken me?"

Thankfully, I never, ever felt that. Others felt it for me, I think. They said they wouldn't blame me if I was angry with God, but I wasn't.

After a November 2006 plane crash in Lexington, Kentucky, killed all aboard but the co-pilot, I was so incredibly shocked to see on my AOL pop-up news that his first words upon seeing his family in the hospital were, "Why would God do this to me?" I prayed so hard for that guy that day. The media was wrong to have reported that and the backlash was scathing. But in reading the comments posted, it was apparent that not a single critic had ever been in a near death experience, or even in excruciating pain or let alone be the sole survivor of a catastrophic tragedy. No one had walked in our shoes. I wrote the pilot a letter.

Though I didn't share his feelings, I had shared his experience. That guy needed a friend.

Morning after morning the staff psychiatrist would come in for a visit. He was a native of India. A small man who with his good intentions and singsong voice would always ask the same two questions: "Do you fell like harming yourself today?" and "Do you feel guilty for being alive?"

Even before I could clearly think, I always answered "No." I couldn't imagine where he was coming from. I couldn't even feed myself and had strangers brushing my teeth. With what heart monitor wire would I fashion a knot for a makeshift gallows? What IV needle already stuck in me as far as it could go would I remove to cut my wrist? Harming myself? Not going to happen.

I already hurt too badly.

The future wasn't going to include adding more pain; it was going to be a plan to erase the existing pain.

The "guilty for being alive" part though; I couldn't even begin to wrap my head around what he was asking. But what I was to learn was that he wasn't off base in asking. He was just early.

The only thing that got me through all of it was faith. And that is the topic I need to address in this chapter. For those of you who are non-believers in the power of prayer or the presence of a real God, not just a "higher power," just skip to the next chapter because this one is so deeply personal and so essential to the story of my survival, that I'm going to end up offending you as some evangelist and you won't finish the book.

If you are believers of any denomination, you will nod in understanding and hopefully read of His healing as evidence of His existence. He had a plan for Michael Nolte, and it included a good future and one of hope. I've learned the "hope" part wasn't just for me, but now for others as well.

I come from non-stop generations of Roman Catholics. I was born at St. Luke's Hospital in Kansas City, Missouri, December 9, 1954. I was baptized at St. Augustine's Catholic Church. I was enrolled in Catholic grade school where I received the sacraments. I participated in outdoor May crownings and jostled for the spots on the altar boy schedule (having moved from Kansas City to Chamois at the end of the fifth grade, I never made it to the big time, i.e., funerals and weddings, as that was a privilege reserved only for the eighth graders). Every day began with an all school Mass. Every class began with prayer. My faith was molded by my teachers.

When the intercom announced in Mr. Nelles' geography class that the president had been shot, I closed the mustard-colored book with the globe on it and joined all the fourth graders on my knees as we prayed the rosary.

When the month to honor the Blessed Virgin would roll around, Mom would help Sherry and me set up a little Mary altar in our living room. The statue of Mary was a First Communion gift from my maternal grandmother. A dresser scarf crocheted by my Dad's Aunt Minnie Wolz was our altar cloth. My parents had received it as a wedding gift.

We had money for little. I mean money...for little...but they made sure we had money for a family Bible. And it was on the coffee table all the time. I think it was the most luxurious home accessory they owned with its gilded pages and full color reproductions of Old Masters religious paintings.

When we moved to Chamois, I got a new slant on Catholicism as we were related to much of the town and most of it was Catholic. Having so many relatives buried in the Catholic cemetery gave me a sense of "This is from whence I came." Not being Catholic was as foreign to me as the concept of not going to college.

Living just blocks from the two-room school and church (both having been attended by my parents), I was frequently recruited to run errands for the nuns, Sister Mary Ludger, Sister Francella Marie, Sister Priscilla, and St. Angelica, all School Sisters of Notre Dame. Likewise my family would help ready the convent in August as the nuns returned from their Motherhouse in St. Louis. Both my parents maintained extremely close relationships with nuns as children and in appreciation, they received our respect 24/7. Anything the sisters would even hint at needing done, Dad was right there.

The pastor, Father A.J. Grellner, had married my parents and was eventually at the post of Most Pure Heart of Mary Church for almost 32 years. He lived in the rectory like a hermit but did tremendous good for all the community. He depended on me to help ready the church for feast days and decorate it for holidays (a precursor to my career). I served Mass, including the big-time ones, until I was a senior in high school. Upon his departure, he gave me two of the Latin books no longer used at Mass and his personal chalice and ciborium. Both are in our living room now.

Together Fr. Grellner and I would travel Osage County posting flyers about the annual church picnic, always the last Sunday of July. (Why we didn't mail them I'll never know.) Likewise he and I would purchase all the prizes for bingo and order the chickens and ground beef for the dinner. I was just a kid! And yet he relied on me like an adult. I'm humbled now, by his respect for my emerging maturity. It probably helped it considerably.

Though I know there are indeed abuses of that office, Father Grellner was a genuine humble servant and priest. I never saw him relax even to the point of removing his Roman collar. He would walk the block around the church, rectory, school, and convent each evening reading his Divine Office. Regardless of the mid-Missouri heat, he would be in his cassock. And of course no air conditioning in his house...or the convent...or the church...or the school.

I mention the above as illustration of how I saw faith worked into daily life. I was immersed with belief without needing to go on a quest. I never understood the concept of being saved, to which the Protestants referred. How could you go from one day not being deserving of heaven and then in one emotionally motivated frenzied experience be told you're now worthy and then go back to your normal sinful life and still believe that you had achieved your pass to salvation? I saw my spiritual journey always as one of a process, not reaching a graduation point.

The graduations that I knew of happened in 8th grade, high school, and college. They marked the conclusion of an experience.

Chamois, Missouri, with all of its 658 (in 1969) residents had six churches, two funeral homes and two schools: public K -12 and Catholic 1-8th. The Catholic school had been reduced from its larger operation of an upstairs auditorium, basement lunchroom, and three classrooms to just two working classrooms, when I enrolled in sixth grade. Grades first through fourth were taught all together in "The Little Room" and fifth through eight were down the corridor in "The Big Room." The mostly neglected center room served as a catch-all and media room.

I don't know if it was decreasing enrollment or a decreasing availability of nuns, but mine was the last class of graduates to walk in a Commencement Mass, May 25,1969. In celebration, the nine of us bought boutonnières for the boys and corsages for the girls. We even ordered a corsage for Sister Mary Ludger who was kind enough to pin it to her habit (though much against the rules I later learned). When the nuns left that summer, it was the end of an era for Chamois. All future Catholic students attended the public school and religion was taught through the lay people in a program know as |the Confraternity of Christian Doctrine (C.C.D.). My mother was the second graders' teacher, preparing them for First Communion, for more than 25 years.

In high school, we formed a very active Catholic Youth Organization (C.Y.O.) and sponsored fundraisers and dances through all four years. On Fridays after school we even had a Teen Mass, complete with teens having all the roles of scripture reading, ushering and best yet, the singing. Nowadays that would be called Liturgy Planning. To us, it was a good time. A good way to meet girls from other towns and loosely stay connected to our faith, I guess. We never yielded a nun, priest, or monk out of the group, but none of us ever ended up in prison either. (Maybe there's a balance there.)

In college, I belonged to the campus group named for Saint Cardinal Newman, who had done much work with young people in his priestly life. Every campus in the country, I think, has its version of the Newman Center, which serves a lot like the high school C.Y.O.s (and for the same benefits.) As in many ways, I found at college, a lot more people who had shared interests and there really were some adult-level conversations about faith and the struggles of staying on the right path. Especially now that we were without the jurisdiction of our parents and being 21, we were free to make choices.

I dated girls in high school and college that were of all faiths. What did it matter? I wasn't going to marry any of them.

That kind of thinking of course eventually runs it course and the reality is that eventually I might marry one of them. For me, the pressure for commitment was coming from two girls at the same time and I liked it. Weird.

The girls were completely different. Cindy was a good Catholic girl from a loving home. Smart, cute, an only child, and a sorority sister of my sister's. She and her parents really thought good thoughts about me. I was her date to several formals, escort for Homecoming queen candidate, date for her parents' Silver Anniversary. We loved to dance, drink beer, and talk for hours. My friends all loved her. And I liked her a lot.

Donna and I met as attendants in the same wedding. She had not gone to college. She was from recently divorced parents, smoked, her mother hated men and Catholics. She wore too much eye make-up, had a great tan and kissing her was so great I could look past the smoker's breath. (That's a really good kisser.) She made me think and behave in ways that I had never imagined. We had nothing in common, except one thing and I couldn't get enough of her.

Faith was not high on my list of life priorities in those years of exploration. Didn't need to be. I was immortal, invincible, and Catholic.

Fortunately for Cindy, I didn't marry her. And fortunately for me, I didn't marry Donna.

I graduated from college exactly four years after high school, May 25, 1977.

As a post-grad there were bunches of us guys that roomed together in Kansas City, working various jobs and dating lots of girls. Sometimes switching both. It was a halcyon time of hedonism. I loved those years.

Every weekend was a party. Mid week there was a party. For no reason there was a party. Road trips became a party. Life was one party after another and only by God's grace did I survive it. None of us were ever hit with any misfortune. We were allowed to wallow in the world of self-indulgence. I don't regret it. I'm just thankful that I grew out of it. I know contemporaries that still live like that.

Weekend weddings became a regular social event. I was either a member of the bridal party or attending one, multiple times a summer. The concept of commitment took on new identity as I then realized how much simpler it would be if I had a life-mate of matched faith.

Without design or plan, I fell in love with the woman that blended all that I had liked about Cindy and Donna, and she was Catholic. A bonus!

Our Nuptial Mass, May 24, 1980, was in Saints Peter and Paul Catholic Church in Boonville, Missouri. It was her home parish and I had lived there for four years. From that point on, weekly Mass attendance and a growing awareness of our faith became a welcome addition to our lives.

Fast forward to the christenings of our three daughters in the church and the roles I took on at Our Lady of Lourdes Catholic Church in Columbia. Lector, usher, the "decorations" guy, president of parish council, Eucharistic minister, and whatever role the pastor needed filled. I loved it all. I was becoming my dad. Upon our transfer to Leawood, making a connection to Church of the Nativity was a natural first instinct.

We chose to build our house in the parish boundaries so Emma-Lea would be eligible for education at the newly built school. The church was being roofed as my new store was under construction, just down the hill from the fortress of Catholicism on the rise. When she was little, Emma-Lea said she always felt comforted being able to look out of some of the school windows and see "Daddy's store" within walking distance.

Once again I took up the roles in the parish in areas I could lend a hand. It was a young, booming, big parish – 13,000 people. Median age of the parishioners was 13 years old. There were almost 70 specialty groups for every interest and age. If they didn't have it, you could start it. That's how the annual Father/ Daughter Banquet was conceived. I made the mistake of asking after the Father/Son Banquet, what about those of us who have daughters? They that open mouth become chairmen.

One of the groups, The Men of Nativity, was so big on Wednesday mornings that eventually a Thursday evening group was also formed. It was in the intimacy of that group of 8 to 12 of us, that finally, finally, I came to know Christ.

I had lived all my life as a good guy. All my life as a Christian. All my life, not going to jail. All of my life only thinking about this life. In the study of the Bible (first time) and through the mentoring of three guys, Patrick Concannon, Jim Kafka, and Paul Welsh, I finally, finally came to know what I had been missing. This is only the appetizer, the prelude. The banquet and the concert are on the other side.

How does one come to that realization? Probably through lots of ways. It could be an inspirational speaker, i.e., Billy Graham. It could be through introspection and research, i.e., dissatisfaction with the faith of our fathers. I don't think I'm so unique though, that for many of us, faith came when we least expected it and needed it most. Most people call that coincidence, God's mercy. For me God showed His mercy, His grace, His healing power, when I was so burdened by a cross that I couldn't carry it any longer by myself.

❖

"The Lord's mercy often rides
to the door of our heart
upon the black horse of affliction."
...Charles Spurgeon

Even though the move to Kansas City had been Barbie's idea completely, once it came time to follow through with those plans, she didn't want to go. We had lived apart for 14 months as I commuted between the two cities and two stores. She had come to like the self-imposed separation. In her state of post-partum depression, she viewed every stress with new nursing job, building the new house, enrolling in new schools, new neighbors, new city, and new baby as being my fault. She fled many weekends to return to Columbia, leaving me with three little ones. She reneged on most suggestions and promises made to marriage counselors. She refused to go to a doctor to get medication that might help her. Her parents were of no support to our marriage and there wasn't anyone other than me suggesting that her behavior wasn't appropriate. Thus I was the bad guy. The guy to blame.

It would be an entirely different book to tell you of how that crisis resolved itself but thankfully, it did, although not quickly. It took four years. However, when that burden of how to support this unloving wife, stay in the marriage, run my companies, be a good father, and still be faithful to God and our marriage became too heavy, I simply had to swallow my pride and ask for help.

That evening, February 16, 1995, was in the intimacy and confidentiality of the guys I mentioned earlier. When I finally stopped making up stories about "a friend who's having trouble in his marriage" and told them it was me, they lifted me up in prayer and physically laid their hands on my shoulders as they prayed the text that has seen me through many additional horrible moments:

"For our light and momentary troubles are achieving for us a glory
that far outweighs them all,
So I focus my eyes not on what is seen but rather on what is unseen.

For what is seen is temporary, what is unseen is eternal."
II Corinthians 4:17-19

It made all the sense in the world.

That was my conversion experience. That was the night Protestants would say I was saved.

I felt a sense of almost electricity flowing from their hands, through my body. A cathartic cleansing. A lightness replaced the heaviness in my chest. I simply entrusted my worries, my load, my cross, to the One who was strong enough to carry it for me. I knew that if I would just live every day the way He wanted me to, that "fixing" Barbie wasn't going to be the solution to restoring my peace of mind. There is much to say about this experience, but for the sake of keeping *Burned But Not Broken,* to a readable length, I will have to leave it here by saying that the source of the strength I would need in 2003 laying in both a burning field and later for weeks in a Burn Unit ICU was formed in childhood and polished as an adult.

"Like gold that is tested in fire."

God readied me for the worst times of my life – losing Micah, Cathy and the wreck – in ways that at the time I didn't understand or appreciate. Without those mini-trials though, I could not have been a witness for Him when the time came. The implications of the psychiatrist would have been true much quicker without my faith that this too was a part of God's plan for my life. Without God in my life, I'm confident I would have acted on them. It was that bad.

Where does faith fit into my story?

What place did prayer have in the experience?

Where was God through this whole ordeal?

"Faith" was stuffed into the darkest recesses of my psyche and filled them, and thus there was no room for fear.

I had a lifetime of people "stuffing me" by seeing their faith in works and it had imprinted on my mind. I wanted to be a copycat of the goodness that I had seen exhibited by my parents, by the nuns and priests of my education, by the senior citizens with whom I had a love fest. By the time I made full commitment to turning my life over to Him and living it for Him and not for me, there were no empty chambers or nooks where fear could invade my mind. I trusted that whatever was happening to me – while conscious or unconscious – would be in accordance with God's plan for my life. I was never afraid.

Don't get me wrong. I dreaded, I mean dreaded, the tank, and I often said going in, "Father if it be your will, let this cup pass," but I was never afraid. I just knew it was going to be the worst pain I had ever felt – since two days ago. And I knew I was going to have to go through it again in two more days.

I had to have something that made sense about the pain. I wanted to believe that like exercising, "No pain. No gain." But I couldn't see any gain. It was just concentric torture.

(The psychiatrist who treated me later said that burn victims suffer worse post-traumatic stress disorder than a rape victim. For a rape victim, it starts and ends. Then it's over, at least physically. For a burn victim so bad they have to go to the tank, it's the dread of knowing that it will last, in my case two hours, and that when it's done, it will be scheduled to happen again and there's nothing you can do to stop it. And you have no idea of how many times they are going to require you to go back to the tank.)

None of this pain was for any gain. There wasn't enough painkiller to lessen it, though in reality of course it surely did. As I lived second by second to do the "clumping of minutes" trick to my mind, I was keenly aware of living in this moment. And it occurred to me:

Jesus had also been tortured like this. They had stripped off his clothes in front of strangers.

In the scourging, the Romans whipped him with leather lashes tipped with hooks. The lashing ripped off his flesh, piece by piece.

I instantly recalled my Stations of the Cross meditation that stated that some men didn't even live through the scourging because it was so severe.

As the nurses would pull strips of infected skin off my healing scalp and the blood would run down my forehead and between my eyes, I knew that He had someone pound a crown of sharp thorns into His scalp.

Just as I neared the second hour of the debridement, I remembered that He had hung on a cross for not two, but rather three hours and wasn't in a sitting position. All His body weight was hanging from spikes nearly splitting His wrists in half.

As I tried to stand and bear weight just long enough to pivot into the safety of my reclining wheelchair, I remembered that I had learned that as a crucified prisoner was dying, his lungs started filling up with fluid and he tried to stand up straight on the "foot rest" where his feet were nailed. It would alleviate the breathing congestion. Can you imagine trying to stand up on feet that had spikes driven through them too?

What I had swirling in my focus was the contrast that what was happening to me was only akin to what was happening to Him in the pain that was being inflicted.

In my case I had lived 48 years in la-la land with no idea that this was going to happen. Jesus knew from birth that He was going to be murdered and in such an insidious way.

Furthermore, not only did He not have morphine to dull it, but also He could have stopped it at any time! He could have turned those lunatic maniacs, those Biblical Nazis who derived pleasure from watching others' pain, into blocks of salt. He had done it before.

And yet He didn't.

Whereas I knew that if I could just endure the debridement, surgeries and dressing changes, history was on my side. The patient improves.

He knew starting in the Garden of Olives when His best friends wouldn't even stay awake with Him for an hour, that it was going to get really, really bad and soon. He was so filled with dread that He sweat drops of blood. He knew that it wasn't going to improve for Him. He knew He was going to die and not quickly and painlessly like I nearly did.

He was going to have the most excruciating, dragged-out death ever imagined. And yet He did it.

He did it for me.

He did it so that I might have the chance, if I followed 10 simple rules, to end up living in paradise not just for the time allotted on the prize voucher for a tropical vacation, but forever.

Eternity... eternity... eternity... with Micah, with Cathy, with the Mike I had just met. Can you imagine?

Surely, surely I could stand this just one more second.

My pain paled in comparison with His. There's no other way to look at it. Someone had suffered worse than a burn victim. And it was Jesus Christ, the Son of God.

It was in those moments that I offered my pain as a prayer of thanksgiving. I was so in communion with Him spiritually during those debridements because I had a sense of what He had done for me. Wasn't this the least I could do for Him? Rather than blame Him for this misfortune, or curse my luck, why not just realize that right now it couldn't be about me. If it was, I would have been screaming and causing my nurses to have nightmares too.

I needed to take myself out of it. Maybe it was a form of disassociation like a rape victim feels. I stopped thinking of my body being on the bench in the tank and started just thinking with my mind of what His pain had been like and repeating over and over, "Thank you, Jesus. Thank you, sweet Jesus."

There were two more times when I felt akin to Jesus. One was pre-surgery. One was post-surgery. Both were horrible.

The routine for the O.R. staff was to roll me from the holding bay where they had started some anti-anxiety meds, into the chill of the operating room. I would be fully awake.

There they would take off my gown and ask me to crawl from the gurney to the operating table. The room itself looks like a room reserved for lethal injections. (Or perhaps a room reserved for lethal injection looks like an operating room.) This is the room where the worst, the most serious, hospital work is done. Lives are saved or lost in this room. It's a gruesome feeling.

The operating table is narrow and hard and rises like an altar (of sacrifice) in the middle of the brightly lighted room. Either the Valium wasn't enough or I just couldn't take it anymore but in one of the preparations, I balked. I just couldn't do it again. I seemingly had lost count (and it was only a total of eight operations) of the number of times that I had crawled, nude and tubed, onto the "altar" and laid on my back. There the armrests came up; they stretched out my arms and strapped them down. Likewise, the strangers behind masks chatted about their weekend while I lay there feeling exposed and without dignity.

The mental image of Christ being laid on the cross and His arms stretched and secured seared sharply in my mind. I tried to give thanks for that indignity that He suffered too, but I just couldn't. I rolled back onto the gurney and started to cry. I asked them if they could do me a favor and just put me out while on the gurney. I apologized as I realized that it meant they would have to lift and transfer me to the operating table with no help from the patient, but I was spent. I just couldn't stand the replay of my mini-cross-mounting anymore.

The staff was very sensitive and offered that process for the ones that followed as well. (Surely someone had to have written that in my chart, as it was a different team many days.)

Another time that there was almost an out of body connection to Christ was as I revived to consciousness after one of the operations. I was alone in the recovery room.

As I became aware of the fact that I had unfortunately not died in this operation either, that fact was quickly confirmed with the immediate, intense pain caused by the cutting away of new layers of skin to transplant onto my legs, the debridement of the dead tissue, and the stapling of the skin grafts to my open wounds of legs, feet, soles, hand. The exposed bone in my right leg had been drilled once again in hopes of drawing blood marrow into its rock-like texture. Someone had forgotten to load the IV poles with painkillers. I was brought to full consciousness without the benefit of any morphine.

I screamed so loudly, that all the department staff came running into my bay. The pain was so out of control that it was impossible to bring under control. My teeth were chattering and my body was in a seizure as I twisted and thrashed like a fish impaled on a harpoon. I begged the nurses to allow Barbie into the bay. They refused. I told them that she was a nurse too and that she would be okay with it. They told me they didn't want her to see me like this. I told them I needed her to be with me. Please, please go get her in the waiting room. They refused, until the breakthrough pain had started to let up. It was the single worst pain I felt in the entire experience.

When Barbie finally was able to stand by my bed and hold my right hand, I could barely stop gnashing my teeth to tell her, "There's not enough money in the world that Ford is going to pay me, to make this worth it." She started to cry as well and replied, "I completely agree and though Ford will pay, they'll never know what they've caused."

My anger at Ford Motor Company was so intense at that moment that the only way I could get through it was to recall that Jesus had undeservedly been tortured as an innocent civilian as well. And yet, He even said, "Forgive them Father. They know not what they do." I never got there with Ford. They knew what they were doing. I wasn't the first burn victim their exploding gas tanks had caused to suffer this way.

An earlier burn victim was a trooper from Arizona. His Crown Victoria had also blown up and caused him horrific facial burning. He also lived but looked like he was wearing a mask. (Ford eventually settled his civil suit, and as a part of the settlement, he could not talk about the experience any longer.)

The evening prior to my next surgery, a new anesthesiologist, Dr. Popple, came in to introduce herself and ask if I had any concerns about the surgery the next morning. When I told her of my recovery room horror, she blanched and told me that she was newly re-located from Arizona where she had treated the trooper that had been so severely burned as well. Without re-telling of details, she assured me that she had been witness to his pain levels and gave me her promise to personally supervise both my going under and awakening. I found out later that she did so on her day off. She promised me that I would never have that painful experience again, and I didn't. I thanked God multiple times for once again placing the right people at the right time, in my life.

Above: Last vacation (Still able to wear shorts!)

Left: Our wedding day May 24, 1980

Above: Most Pure Heart of Mary Catholic Church, Chamois, Missouri, home to six generations of Noltes. Left: Sister Mary Ludger, S.S.N.D. , my 6th - 8th grade teacher who helped shape my values and prepared me for my career. Right: Emma-Lea and I at her first communion, 1995.

Top photo: Happy night in Atlantic City! Debbye Turner crowned Miss America 1990. Above: My family of origin on my parents' Golden Anniversary Feb. 16, 2002. The last time we were all together.

Above: All smiles at daughter Caroline's first communion 2001. (Keiser Studio)

Left: Justine's first communion 1997. (Wynn Studio)

Left: Just doing my job.
(The *Kansas City Star*)

Above: With best buddies Phil Molina (l) and Steve Heeney (r).

Top photo: The media called ours a "Norman Rockwell" home. It does have a bit of a Christmas card feel...

Above: My last photo with Micah.

Left: Cathy Isgrig: We loved her THIS much!

Below: July 5, 2002: The worst day of my life. My sister Sherry & husband Tom watch their daughter's casket being loaded into the hearse. Directly behind them, I am holding my godchild Ashley.

Right: Trooper Micheal L. Newton, End of Watch May 22, 2003, at age 25.

Left: Trooper Micheal Newton's tombstone, Newburg, Missouri.

Top photo: My side of the Crown Victoria. (The *Kansas City Star*)

Above: The patrol car arrives in Jefferson City for the vehicle autopsy: remnants of a faulty fuel tank's filler neck. (The *Kansas City Star*)

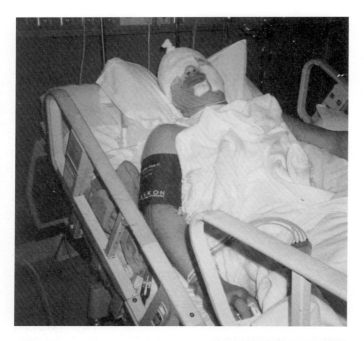

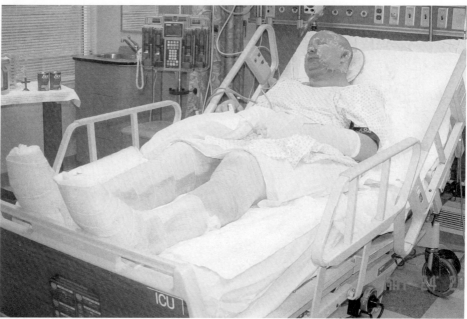

Top photo: Day one of the journey.
Above: In a coma-like state for 13 days. (DBJ)

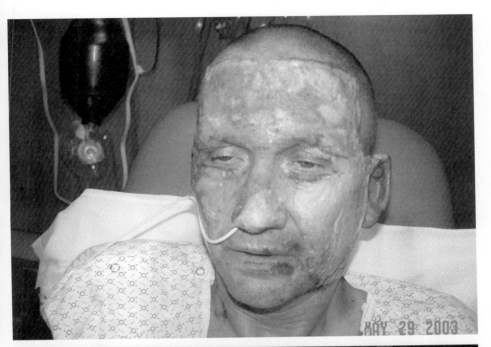

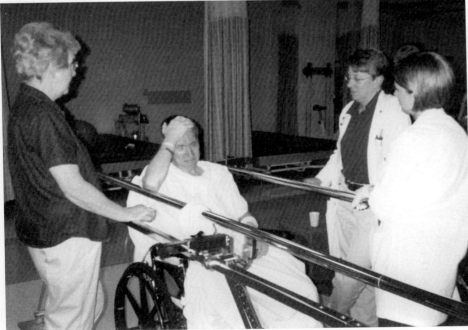

Top photo: In a drugged stupor and unrecognizable to my family, I began to heal. (DBJ)

Above: Emotions run high at the first acceptance of my disability (l to r) Mom, Cathy and Corie were helpless.

Top photo: Me with my Good Samaritans! David Bryan (l) and (r) Troy Brinkoetter.
Above: Providing my lifesavers with a glimpse of their daughters as brides. My treat! (Chuck Cantor)

Above: Barbie trying to express her appreciation to friends after receiving her "Purple Heart."

Left: The toaster cake at Heroes and Angels represented a significant decision on my bounce-back day.

Above: Me and my girls at the conclusion of our Heroes and Angels party.

Left: My visit with Shonnie and Tyler Newton, April 2006.

Top photo: Making up for lack of pigment, a daily chore. (The *Kansas City Star*)

Above: May 2006, I received the Hope and Sprit Award from The University of Missouri Hospital. I was joined by my beloved Dr. Terry and nurse Kandra Voshage. (University of Missouri Hospital)

Top photo: Laying a wreath at the crash site, Mile Marker 47, an annual promise.. (Allison Long/*Kansas City Star*)
Above: Senator Jim Talent and I celebrate the "Pass With Care" law now making the highways safer for law enforcement.

SEVEN
God Was There Even If Father Al Was Ordered Out

Where was God in all this awfulness?

I never asked that question directly, but after reflection, I can see the answers quite clearly.

God was present for me in the kindness of others. And the kindnesses that were extended to me were so generously offered that I know they were God's whisper into the ears of friends.

"Mike really needs (fill in the blank). I need you to do it for Me."

One of the most striking examples of the power of prayer happened during my dressing changes.

After I had graduated beyond having to go to the tank so often, some of the lighter debridement could happen during a dressing change. These changes were staged in my bed and were sort of like a mini-operation of their own.

My legs were wrapped in multiple layers of shredded silver, Xero-flo medicated tissue, gauze, and Ace wrap bandages. The bed was readied with a sterile sheet placed below the legs and everyone in the room would be covered with gowns, hats, masks, and of course gloves. Infection is the greatest threat to a burn victim. To remove all these layers of protection on my legs was always a risk, not to mention painful.

The "taking down," treating, and re-wrapping my legs took about two hours. This was done every other day as well. Though the pain level here was not as bad as the tank (nothing is as bad as the tank) it still required a lot of concentration and induced a lot more pain. As an added precaution to avoid amputation, Dr. Terry ordered a wound vacuum placed on my right leg. It was a suction device attached to my ankle with a black rubber plate. Consistent sucking action pulled out infection and encouraged the downward flow of blood marrow. Within a day, the black rubber had adhered to my flesh and tearing it off caused so much pain that they put me under in a process called conscious sedation.

With conscious sedation, the morphine was ramped up and I was given non-stop boluses of Versed. It was to create an instant amnesia. So as crazy as that sounds, I was feeling the pain, but instantly forgetting the feeling. Paul would administer the drug via syringe into my IV. It was not uncommon for us to go through 10 vials of morphine or Fentynl in two hours.

Two nurses would work on one leg at a time – one holding the leg off the bed, in whatever place she could find that wasn't burned too badly while the other nurse did the unwrapping. The holding nurse had to constantly change positions of her hands to accommodate the un-spiraling. It occurred to me that if I could hold my leg up myself, they could both be unwrapping. When I asked if that was okay to try, they didn't think my weakened quads or lower ligaments would support it but permitted me to try.

I tried. And I could! It was an abdominal strain, but I could do it. I could lift my leg off the mattress and the unwrapping (and then re-wrapping) gained a lot of speed.

When I mentioned this feat to someone from my home parish, they put out a request for additional prayers for me specifically at 2 p.m. when the dressing changes began. Without me knowing they had done this, a week later, I felt an unexpected strength in being able to hold my legs up. The abdominal pain was gone and I was doing leg lifts for 45 minutes at a stretch. (Keep in mind this was the same guy that when invited to join his daughter for yoga on the floor at home couldn't do a leg lift for five minutes!)

The sensation of being lifted up in prayer was exactly that. I could literally feel the buoyancy. I felt as if my shoulders weren't really touching the sheets. It was as if I was on an air raft on the pool. I had a sense of floating. I really couldn't imagine what was causing this, but I decided to try it eventually with both legs, and I found I could do that too. Two legs at one time, off the mattress for 45 minutes. Later I learned that the prayer chain of Nativity had interfaced with the prayer chain of a close Methodist church requesting prayers at 2 p.m. the same day that I tried the dual-leg lift. Coincidence? Or God-incidence? The spiritual aspects aside, once I could hold my own legs aloft, we shaved 30 minutes off the procedure.

God was there.

Representing the faith of my church was my friend and pastor, Father Al Rockers.

Father Al had been notified within minutes of Barbie calling two friends after the patrol called her. As Caroline came into the church for the last day of school Mass, he sought her out and asked if she would mind if he talked about her Dad and requested prayers. She really had no conception of how critically I needed those prayers, but in all her fifth grade wisdom, she agreed. (All this within 30 minutes of the wreck.)

Father Al stayed closely connected by phone to Barbie for several days before he could get away to come see me. He recalls (to my embarrassment) that after he had driven two hours to get there, he was admitted into my Bed One cubicle only to be ordered out. I was completely out of my head with painkiller and when he spoke to me, I replied by saying, "You have to leave right now. I'm going to have a B.M."

So he left.

I've since asked him if the second half of that action really happened and he chuckled and said, "I don't know, I was ordered out." Four hours of driving for a three-minute visit!

In spite of my rudeness, Father Al continued to call at least once a week. As I became more lucid, I also became more aware of pain. I felt there were people in the Burn Unit worse off than me. I could hear them moaning. I didn't think I should vocalize what I was feeling. Father Al was the one who validated my pain and helped me make sense of the situation.

He asked, "Mike, is your pain just excruciating all the time?"

I admitted it to him, "Yes, Father, it is. I hurt so much I can't even pray through it."

He then told me of St. Thomas Aquinas who wrote, "A hungry man cannot pray until his hunger has been satiated." He said I should not beat myself up over not being able to pray but rather to offer my pain up as my prayer. Such a simple thought, but I hurt so much I couldn't think of it on my own. After that conversation, I felt that I was okay with God. He was cool with the reality that right now, formal prayer – prayer as I had always known it – just wasn't going to happen.

God was there.

My guy friends are usually rather slow to subtlety, so I'm assuming God used more than a whisper when He told my two buddies, Steve Heeney and Phil Molina, "Mike needs you, but in small doses."

Steve, Phil, and I had been meeting on Thursday evenings for a number of years following our attendance at a Promise Keepers conference in which men were encouraged to invest in a relationship called "Accountability Partners." With the premise of keeping each other on the straight and narrow, we often deviated to the crooked and crazy path of having a good time. We would go sailing on Steve's boat, drink beer in my garage while watching it rain, help raise each other's kids, support each other through our wives' expectations, read a couple of really helpful books, attend a bunch of black-tie events together, barbecue, grab lunch a couple times a month, and in general just be there for each other.

To date the crises that had come our way included the unexpected passing of Steve's mother and the much-expected divorce that Phil's wife initiated. Phil even lived with us in two segments of time, as the divorce was raging. When Micah was killed, Phil came to her funeral. Steve and I learned a lot about the process of grieving as we compared notes on how he had processed losing a member of his family and what I was feeling in my own experience.

They are terrific friends.

As soon as they learned of the wreck, they met up and together they rushed to Columbia. Phil was quoted later by a reporter that the only way he knew the figure laying in the bed was his friend Michael Nolte is that the distinctive crook in my little finger was still uncovered and that was recognizable. They stayed with Barbie a long time that night.

The "small doses" part was what I valued and needed the most. They would come after working all day, just as visiting hours were ending. The nurses would allow them to pull the curtain and remain for as long as I needed them. Sometimes it was 1 a.m. before that need was met. Quietly and without having to be on, I could articulate my thoughts about what was happening to me. Theirs were the visits that brought relaxation and resolve. It dawned on me later, that they didn't return home until 3 a.m. and then worked all the next day.

Phil was the one I asked to drive me home from the hospital and he literally carried me into my house. Steve was the one that I asked to drive me to the sentencing of Paul Daniel and, emotionally, he carried me through that horrible day. Both of these guys did their own Simon of Cyrene imitation better than I could ever do it.

God was there.

While at Central Missouri State University, I lived three years in the same room, 412 of South Ellis Hall. It was a dorm full of great guys all looking for the same thing each weekend – a great party. (And whatever came with it.)

I lived in the same room for such a long time, because I was having such a good time. One of the guys who brought color to the memories of those days was David Akin. Akin (and his roommate Dave Moore or "Moore" as he was always known) were inseparable since high school and maintained that friendship as roomies through college. Akin was what the girls would now call eye candy, with great hair. What they didn't know is that he was just a kid at heart who would act like a crazy man when he was drunk and still act that way when he was sober. Seeing Akin air-guitaring in his underwear in the hallway was so commonplace, we didn't even look up anymore.

After moving to Kansas City, the hometown of lots of college friends, I tried to get a reunion together in celebration of the 21st anniversary of my 21st birthday. (That had been a night to remember for all of us!) Though I hadn't seen him in years, he wrote me a scathing note declining the invitation. He wrote that we had nothing in common except four years of behavior for which he now regretted. He had become a member of a fundamentalist church and they encouraged him to shed all his old ways. Participating in this reunion would only bring him shame. I was astonished. Akin?!!!

Greater astonishment six years later when the Burn Unit receptionist notified me of a visitor requesting admission. It was a "Mr. Akin." Akin? There could only be one! But I heard he was in Houston. What in the world?

In walked Mr. Eye Candy Akin, now with a full head of Stone Phillips silver hair. It had been 24 years since we had seen each other.

He had received a call from Moore who still lived in Kansas City. He couldn't let me die without asking me to forgive him for the insulting way he replied to my invitation to a birthday party reunion. He drove all the way from Texas to see me. His sincerity brought tears to my eyes and his. The forgiveness was easily granted and the visit was one that merited a photograph to be taken. I told him at this rate, the next time we would see each other, we would be 72.

God was there.

The business still had business. But the owners were both 100 miles away for more than two months. One was in bad shape.

Businesses have overhead that doesn't go away just because the owner's been burned, unless your landlords are George Lieberman and Jeff Alpert.

Of all the calls that Barbie couldn't take on that first day, one that she did was from them. Jeff expressed concern from both himself and George and said words that she says she'll never forget, "Barbie, the most important thing for you to think about is getting Mike through this. Don't even think about the stuff that doesn't matter, like the rent. As of today, the rent stops period. We'll talk about it later if and when you feel you can pay it again."

Within two weeks of discharge, I had my niece Ashley drive me to their offices so I could say "thank you" in person. I'm confident that they suspected their secretary Val had made a typo when she set an appointment with Mr. Nolte and they expected Mrs. Nolte. They probably thought she was coming to tell them she was closing down the store. When the door opened and I rolled in, they could barely contain their astonishment or composure. I thanked them. Oddly I told them of the hallucinations. They are Jewish men and if anyone would understand that atrocity, they would. They didn't know what to say. They did say they didn't expect the rent to be re-paid. I insisted.

It took us awhile, but we did re-pay it, with interest (my insistence).

God was there.

A book this size could be filled with similar stories. Stories of truth. Stories of kindness. Stories that inspire me to be a friend, like people have demonstrated friendship to me.

The days rolled into weeks, the weeks rolled into months. My ability to walk was progressing. The tubes and wires were being removed slowly: the central line, the feeding tube, the Foley catheter, the heart electrodes, the IV. Finally, one day I was tube free. Frightening almost. What if I needed something fast?

The IVs were the worst. My parents knew that drug use in college would never be a temptation, as I hated needles so much. Even when I would have to have a blood draw for routine tests or health insurance reasons, I would lay on the floor to save falling on to it. Now every three days a big IV needle was being stuck into a vein either on the soft tissue of my underarm or the back of my hand. I dreaded the IV team doing it the most. So many infiltrated veins. So much bruising and burning.

Knowing it was IV change day and how much I hated it, Kandra offered to do it for me. She worked in my elbow area for several minutes and had three punctures. She was so frustrated with herself that she finally agreed to let it go one extra day. My veins were becoming impossible to penetrate. The blood transfusions helped my responsiveness, but didn't restore my veins.

Each night I was given a shot of blood thinner in the stomach. Little needles. Big stress. One night a temp nurse dressed like an Elvis impersonator delivered the shot. He tore the skin on my stomach so badly I slept with hot packs on the site all night. He was never hired back again.

The evenings in the unit were the loneliest. Typically as visiting hours ended, the nurses became less busy as patients started to fall asleep. I could overhear their talk of normal lives. Of their weekends, their families, their lives outside the unit. I couldn't relate to any of that anymore. I couldn't even imagine it anymore.

I had begged my parents and family to all go home. It was now more than 50 consecutive days that they had been away from home. My daughters were scattered all across the state, staying with various relatives and friends. I had missed Justine's dance recital and she spent the week of performance at the home of her friend and fellow dancer Lauren Thompson. Mrs. Thompson drove the girls to and from all the practices, and Dr. Thompson asked if Justine wanted him to dance with her in the "Father Daughter" opening number. She said, "No thank you." It was a sad week for her.

As much as Caroline stayed with the Adrians all the time, being required to stay with the Adrians put it in a completely different light. Marie Adrian (aptly named for the Blessed Mother, because she is one herself) did everything she could to keep things normal for Caroline. A time that a daughter really needs her mom, though, is as she adjusts to sudden physical changes and Barbie wasn't there for this critical time that summer.

Emma-Lea kept Barbie company much of the time. She would stay in the waiting room with my parents through much of the day if Barbie was in my room with me. Their days revolved around my surgeries, my visitors, gifts being delivered, old friends showing up, new friends being made. At one point the stress of it all triggered Emma-Lea to go into a full body tetany. This condition of paralysis is caused by a rare kidney condition she has called Gitelman's Syndrome. Barbie dealt with that medical emergency just as I was being rolled out of recovery.

To further complicate things, my father suffered a gall bladder attack in the waiting room as well that landed him five days as a patient on 5 West. By that time I was portable, and Barbie would wheel me up to Dad's room where we would all just sit and stare at each other in disbelief that this was actually happening. One hospital having two Mr. Noltes as patients? Barbie and Mom swore they were going to "run off and nobody will ever find us" when this was over.

There was always some drama playing out either in the waiting room, in the unit or within the dynamics of my extended family.

Though I was on anti-anxiety medication, sleep often would elude me. It was during those late, late hours, that peace would often settle into my chest. It would be past midnight and the lights dimmed, inside and out. My shots were done, my day gown replaced with a nightgown, the room cleaned up and I was left alone. Sometimes I would re-read a stack of cards. Often times I would turn on the television.

The last television watching I ever scheduled was *30 Something* and *Dallas.* From then on I never sat still long enough to watch popular shows. I seldom got any of the jokes made famous by comedy or commercials. To watch television after midnight is to see only the re-runs (except if you never saw them before). It's all brand new. I watched episode after episode of

Seinfeld, Everybody Loves Raymond, Will and Grace and really, really late at night, *Golden Girls.* That pattern affected me for months afterward as now I often don't feel like I can sleep, unless I'm watching one of those shows. Weird.

The grafts were holding. If the hole in my leg would just seal shut with the next surgery, I could leave the hospital.

Dr. Terry performed the surgery and then left a few days for his 50th class reunion in Utah. While he was gone, all hell broke loose under the guidance of his possible successor. (In the interest of not maligning her reputation for wherever she is now practicing, she will only be referred to as Dr. M.)

Dr. M. was charged with my care and to make the final decision as to my being discharged. In retrospect, I know I had lobbied too hard for this transition and should have not been released when I was. I think she bought into my bravado and declared me fit. She said I was too young to be so disabled and she prescribed an aggressive regimen of out of home rehab and called the rehab center in Leawood to set it up for the week I came home. The graft was barely sticking to my leg but it was "up-and-out-time" in her mind.

On my mother's birthday, Dr. M. pronounced me eligible for discharge the following day. Mom said it was the best present she could have received. My P.T. and O.T. were horrified at the determination and told me to ignore everything Dr. M. was prescribing. I was told to remember that I hadn't been out of bed in 10 weeks and she wants me out of the house, three times a week? I did as they told me and waited for Dr. Terry's return to discuss a more gradual rehab that wouldn't be so potentially damaging.

The day before I was discharged was filled with a roller coaster of emotions.

Two of my lawyers came again to see me. (I wasn't conscious the first time they visited.) So for me it was the first time to meet them. The conversation was very stilted, as I didn't understand the first thing about filing a lawsuit against a Fortune 500 company. I was interested in replacing my totaled car and getting back to work. They told me to not do either until all the factors were considered in regard to the trial. I asked when that would take place and they said "in about two years."

I soaked in what they said as "Don't drive. Don't go to work. For two years." I lost it. They just sat there and looked at me uncomfortably. All of this was made even more uncomfortable as this firm was also representing Micah's parents in their suit against Union Pacific. They had just come out of a tough meeting with Sherry and Tom in a hospital conference room. When they pulled themselves together in the privacy of the conference room, they came to visit me and found me doing what they just finished. It started all over.

In the middle of that scenario, the social worker popped her head in my curtain and joyfully said, "Good news Mr. Nolte. Your wheelchair will be waiting for you when you return home tomorrow!"

Good news? Who in the hell wants a wheelchair to be waiting for them when they get home? When I go home, it's because I'm better. If I'm better, then that means I don't need a wheelchair. Take your damn wheelchair and just shove it up...

The lawyers left. The Starkes left. And I became hysterical.

I called my friend Bill Oades. He is the leader of our Men of Nativity group and each Tuesday would call the hospital for a progress report before the next morning's meeting. Beyond that though, Bill and I have shared many similar worries of being self-employed. He owns Goodyear stores. He and his wife Peggy have been special people in our lives since our years as "Soup Group" friends – a "Fridays of Lent" group that gathered for just soup, and continued with monthly dinner parties for years.

If anybody could relate to the news of being told that you couldn't go back to work for two years, it would be Bill. And of course that wasn't what the lawyers were saying and Bill realized that. He was both good listener and advisor. And he really got the brunt of the "wheelchair waiting" remark.

That night, I couldn't stop crying. I think the emotional gauntlet of Dr. M, the lawyers, Barbie out of town, the realization that tomorrow I was sailing out of safe harbor, just became too much. I spent part of the night writing thank you notes to each of my 31 nurses and finally, finally fell asleep. I had to get some sleep, because tomorrow Debbye was coming. It was my get-away day.

❖

Debbye Turner, the pride of the city, the state and particularly the University of Missouri.

Debbye was my third Miss Columbia to be crowned Miss Missouri and four months later, Miss America. Our daughters sat in fascination as she practiced the marimba in our living room preparing for the talent competition of the scholarship pageant. She was the complete package: smart, glamorous, charismatic and talented. When she made history for our state, Barbie and I were in the audience in Atlantic City as she took her walk as Miss America 1990. At the end of the runway, she looked right into the camera and mouthed the words, "I love you Columbia!" I was under a dog pile of Debbye fans that just went nuts.

After the press conference, we were invited to the Presidential Suite of Trump Tower for an intimate reception. I chatted with "the Donald" on the escalator to that over-the-top collection of rooms filled with roses, champagne, and Godiva chocolates. The suite was ready for the newly crowned Miss America who would be sleeping there. During the course of her reign, Debbye toured the country espousing her platform to young people, "If I can become this, you can do whatever you set your mind to." People loved her. I accompanied her on a couple of appearances and orchestrated a three-day, citywide homecoming celebration in her honor. It was a heady year.

After taking her final walk, she crowned her successor, Miss Illinois, who also wore a gown I had custom designed. I was so "Miss America'd out" I opted to not go, but Barbie was there for her (a decision I regret to this day).

Debbye returned for her delayed senior year and received her doctor of veterinary medicine degree. We hosted her graduation party at our house. She and Cathy Isgrig sat together at Caroline's christening reception and became very good friends.

Debbye's popularity as a motivational speaker continued for years and landed her a job as a correspondent with The Early Show on CBS. She reluctantly left St. Louis where she had lived a number of years anchoring a local talk show but found the Big Apple exciting and comfortable.

Debbye and I had a long friendship. When her mother Gussie died unexpectedly, Barbie and I drove 13 hours to the funeral in Arkansas. When I founded the Father/Daughter Banquet for my church, I invited her to be our first celebrity speaker and she accepted. The after-dinner entertainment included both an edited tape of her pageant successes and a musical video collage of all the fathers and daughters in attendance. I had asked her father, Fred, in Texas, to help me surprise her with a snapshot of the two of them as the last photo in the montage. Debbye was watching from the front row and was caught completely off guard by the finale.

I've never seen her so "got." To be included in such a personal way. When she came to the microphone, it was the first and only time I've seen her flustered.

And now Debbye was coming to see me in this dismal state and share my lowest moment. She flew from New York to St. Louis in the pre-dawn hours and rented a car for the two-hour trip to Columbia. When the Burn Unit staff found out she was coming, there was a buzz in the hospital. As the hour of her arrival neared, housekeeping needed me out of my room as a new arrival was headed to take my place. As Barbie was outside getting her tutorial and a ream of pain killer prescriptions, Debbye arrived. She gave Barbie a quick hug and said, "Where is he?" She had no time for admirers. She politely excused herself and followed Barbie's pointed finger.

She had flown all that way and we had about 20 minutes of private time. She brought me Godivas and note cards. We prayed briefly together and she pushed me to the elevator as I made my way to the lobby. There the Columbia media and friends had assembled to see me off. Kandra and Corie, both off that day, had come in to say good-bye. I asked Kandra to do the ceremonial snipping of the patient I.D. bracelet that I had worn for more than two months and I presented gifts of flowers and Brighton jewelry to them and left the same for Cathy who was on vacation.

"Can't stop....can't talk," I yelled as Debbye pushed my wheelchair towards the elevator.

Debbye joyfully sang of praise and worship and everyone joined in the clapping as she wheeled myself out to the waiting van. Thirty pounds lighter, pale, burr hair, legs bandaged and horizontal, but I was going home!

Phil had created a soft nest of air mattresses and pillows for the long journey back to Kansas City. We were about to reverse the trip I started to take 10 weeks ago.

As I left the hospital, I mistakenly thought the bad times were behind me.

EIGHT
The New "Normal"

"There's no place like home. There's no place like home."

Familiar words, spoken by another Kansan, though fictional, in reality, had an element of truth in them.

I was about to return to a place where I had been for many years. It wouldn't have changed. What I didn't realize is that though the house hadn't changed, the homeowner had.

As we headed west, home to Leawood, Kansas, it was surreal on many levels. First, I wasn't driving my own vehicle. Secondly, I was lying horizontal (to minimize the pain in my legs). And lastly, I was about to ride by the setting for the tragedy that shaped the rest of my life – Mile Marker 47.

The local media had been checking periodically with the hospital to get updates on my condition. Though that information was guarded, they did learn of the day I was discharged, and the phone started ringing.

Barbie took the calls while Phil drove. My attorneys guided her to a compromise of letting the news stations film from the street, but that I was not to make a comment... period.

As we approached the scene of the wreck, Phil slowed a little at my request. Though from the other side of the highway, I viewed the scorched earth, the huge white cross, the flags and the wreaths. Though I couldn't remember exactly where on the highway I had been pulled over, all of a sudden even the width of the shoulder looked familiar. I could feel myself coasting to a stop and pulling off the highway as far as I could to give Officer Newton as wide a berth as possible. It hadn't mattered.

My stomach convulsed, but I didn't throw up. Home was now only 50 minutes away and I would be coming back and forth on Interstate 70 many, many more days as my post-hospital burn care continued in Columbia.

As we rounded the corner to our cul-de-sac, I was somewhat surprised to see some news cameras standing in the center of the street (not safe). But I was very surprised to see our driveway full of friends and the garage and picket fence wrapped in banners and balloons. I, "Mr. Party," really hadn't expected this and wasn't sure that I really wanted this, but here I was and there they were.

Once the van stopped, the side door popped open and there were several smiling faces eager to help. As would often be the case in coming weeks, friends didn't know where to touch, thus I quickly learned that the awkwardness vanished if I would just verbally tell them what was safe to grab – right hand, waist, bottom of foot if they were in splints (but not if only in bandages). Our friend Mary Pat Sullivan, also an R.N., had the foresight to bring a transfer belt. It was a wide band that cinched around the patient's waist leaving a small tail of leash. Before I knew it, she had me lassoed and tied off. I slowly edged out onto my feet and the assembly cheered as I stood upright.

Though the wheelchair was as promised, "waiting your (my) arrival," I insisted that if I had walked out of that house 10 weeks ago, by gosh, I was going to walk back into it now.

As I have seen some of the saved footage used for the evening news, I realize that the walk was really more of a shuffle, but with the help of my walker – Phil leading and Mary Pat lifting – I made it up the three brick steps and turned to announce the obvious, "I am home!" I was so excited to utter those words that both hands came off the walker as I raised my fists over my head, Rocky style, and promptly lost my balance in the pivot. I stumbled into our familiar foyer with the yellow background botanical wallpaper that I hope Barbie never changes.

The next few hours were spent just basking in the affection of the friends who loved me most. I sat in the recliner with legs elevated and champagne was served all around. Everyone was amazed at the recent return of hair and though short and spotty, some of the ladies would rub my head for good luck! We laughed and laughed.

When the crowd thinned out, the only people I really wanted to unwind with were the ones that had been at the starting gate of this trip with us – the Adrians. Ron and Marie came over in the early evening and stayed until Barbie announced it was my bedtime.

It dawned on us then that the master bedroom was upstairs – up 14 stairs to be exact, with only a handrail on one side of the curving flight. In P.T., I had practiced with a double handrail.

Nothing would do, but Ronnie had Son No. 2, Jonathan, drafted quickly and together, the former quarterback and the present wrestler lifted my now 160 pounds in their basket of arms and we ascended the steps before I could say "No."

Being laid in one's bed is a humbling moment, but made even more so when you realize that you also can't get out of the bed to use the toilet, even with help. The concept of bearing weight on my burned-off soles was so painful that I would break out in a sweat just imagining it. Thus the urinal was still part of my bedroom décor, not on a push-from-view, rolling table, but now further highlighted as it was propped on my bedside table right under the lamp. (Ego, ego, ego.)

After administering the "night meds" of morphine for pain – Remeron for sleep, Xanex for short-term anxiety, Clonipin for long-term anxiety, antibiotic for infection, Celexa for depression, Temazepam for restless leg syndrome, and zinc for new skin growth – I was readied for the night.

For the first time in over two months, I was going to be sleeping with my wife. Initially the concept was a little unnerving as so much of my body had to be propped up on pillows at different points and I couldn't be bumped. When at last we were settled in, we realized that our prayers had been answered. We were back home together. I was alive. The emotion of the moment was a breaking wave. With all my health care clutter, our bedroom looked like a nursing home.

I turned to Barbie and said with honesty, "This is not what you signed up for 23 years ago. This kind of goes beyond 'in sickness and health.' I don't want you to have to put up with this and I would understand if you wanted to leave. I will still give you half the money. (Future lawsuit compensation.) You deserve it."

She looked at me as if I had just grown two heads, "I'm not going anywhere. You're the one stuck with me. But I still want half the money!" She kissed me and said, "Welcome home, bed partner." I slept like a rock.

The next day began the beginning of my new normal. Barbie dressed me for 10:30 Mass and the Adrian men carried me down the steps and laid me in the van. At church, they placed me in my wheelchair and at long last I was allowed into the building that housed the people that had prayed for me for weeks. It was all I could do to not break down as they rolled me in.

Attending the first service after arriving back home was important to me because lying in the burn unit all those weeks, I had visualized walking again...walking down the aisle at the Church of the Nativity, only a mile from our home. I could feel the tile floor beneath my feet. In my dreams, I would stand there a moment, ponder going right or left. I would sense the slope of the floor, pick a pew and, as I sat down, feel the texture of the seat cushion. It was my dream to walk back alive into my church – not my store or my home, but my church.

The decision to attend Mass that morning proved to be the right one. The experience turned out to exceed my expectations although I was never able to leave my wheelchair as I had envisioned.

I wanted to draw as little attention as possible and asked to be positioned to the farthest side against the wall. Behind me was a group of about 25 friends who had gathered there as a gesture of solidarity and support. My anonymity was short lived though as Father Al opened the liturgy with the words, "In our midst is one of our own who has traveled not to hell, but through hell, and back. What he told me he missed most about Mass was the sense of community that we call 'church.' I would like you to join me in not welcoming Michael Nolte back, but welcoming him home."

More than 1,200 people stood up and applauded and looked around for where I might be sitting. I was so overwhelmed that I forgot the technique to release the brake so I might roll forward, become visible for a minute, say "thank you" and roll back. From that point on, my first Mass back was a constant struggle of keeping emotions in check as the choir sang all my favorite hymns and the homily centered on overcoming adversity.

At the distribution of communion, the attendees walk forward with cupped hands to receive the consecrated host. Father Al started this process by walking out into the congregation to present the Body of Christ to me in my wheelchair. When I saw he was making this accommodation, I waved him back and said, "Please stay there. I'm coming to you." Those hours of physical therapy paid off as I lurched from my chair, grabbed my walker and walked the 12 feet, unaided, to receive the Eucharist. It was very, very affirming.

Hoping to not clog up the vestibule with the struggle out of my wheelchair and into the van, I voted to stay put until most of the congregation had exited. However, that quickly became a mess as I was in a narrow aisle and lots of people waited to say a few words. Miserable traffic plan. Wonderful feeling.

I was so not in control – of my day, my life – that I hadn't even thought to ask if we were going to follow our tradition of lunch out. Before I knew it, we were back home, I was propped up in a hearth room chair and the house was filling with people.

Fran Cashion and Ginnie Bono commandeered our kitchen with pots of pasta and wine all around. Like loaves and fishes, there was more and more as people filtered into the house for the impromptu luncheon. I simply sat by the mantel and watched and visited. I relished every single syllable that was spoken.

Barbie eventually made it over to me and asked why I wasn't eating. I replied "No one has brought me a plate." It was one of the many light bulb moments to come: "He's home, but he's different." I couldn't walk through a buffet line. I couldn't carry a plate. Fortunately we both laughed about the oversight and opposed to triggering tears, as we realized that I was indeed disabled. I was physically unable to get my own lunch.

What with the crowds, the volume, the sheer joyful exuberance, I was absolutely spent by late afternoon. I didn't care. It will always be remembered as one of the "Top 10 Happiest Days of My Life." My first full day back home. What a special meaning those words would take as I reflected on the experience.

The next day, Monday, was the beginning of "the revolving door."

Before leaving the ICU, Paul, Dr. Terry's assistant, had cautioned me to make my first week at home just like my last week in the hospital. What did he know? I was H.O.M.E.! No rules. I couldn't wait to see the people that hadn't been allowed into the Burn Unit because of the infection risk. I was just anxious to re-connect with my life, my friends. Barbie left to run the company and my girls started taking calls from visitors. I didn't want to refuse anybody.

My first guest stayed almost two hours! I thought I was going to expire just from sitting up in a chair that long.

After the first few days of non-stop visitors, I came to realize that I had to pace myself. My energy reserve just wasn't there. But what I also came to realize is that for some people the seeing was believing. The reports had been horrifying (truthful, but horrifying). No one knew a burn victim, injured this badly, that had survived. When they came to see me, often they would start crying either from relief that it was still me, or in some cases they needed to process their own story of unresolved grief over a burn injury in their own family.

My friend Michael shared with me the burn injury death of his father when Michael was in junior high school. My friend Bob re-told the story of a car wreck that nearly killed him.

While I had been in the hospital, I received almost 50 cards from one woman alone. She explained that she sent the cards because her brother had also been a burn victim, but since they did not live in the same state, she was never able to visit him in person either.

Each of these people had a profound reverence for my experience and related to it on a level that most, thankfully, could not. I know that their graciousness and many gestures of kindness to my family were to either pay back or pay forward for what they had suffered. I think it's a tremendous gift to be able to let a friend share their story, to process their memories and to accept the outcome of their history. I needed to let them see me and keep silent while they talked. It was humbling.

As business manager, my nurse, and homemaker, the last thing Barbie had time for was preparing dinner. No need to worry. Lynn DeBacco, whose children were in class with ours, arrived onto the "Dinner for the Noltes" scene with a calendar of deliveries and interview questions as to our food allergies and preferences. The burden of meal preparation was lightened for the next four months as people called Lynn to get on the schedule. Unbelievable.

(Lesson to self: When taking a meal to a family in distress, don't use that as catch-up time. Take the meal. Hold back on the bread and dessert, and leave.)

My weeks were organized around our four-hour round trips to University of Missouri Hospital where my beloved Dr. Terry continued for months to treat my wounds. He was concerned about the earlier recommendation for out of the house rehab and reined that concept in for a few months. Each visit to the Burn Clinic was always a self-esteem booster as the staff marveled at my progress in standing and walking.

As the bandages were reduced I was measured for compression garments. These tight tights were so painful to wear that after donning them the first time during a clinic visit, I could barely stand them during the ride home. By 8 p.m., I was writhing in pain and searched for a scissors to cut them off. Six hundred dollars later, there they lay in a shredded heap. I just couldn't take them.

On the next trip to the Burn Clinic, a new pair awaited me and I dreaded the prospect of the adjustment. I felt like a colt being broke. Fate intervened that day though, as I was offered the chance to visit with another burn victim who was six months from date of injury.

Mary, a woman in her 60s, was one of the many that I came to know that felt a little gasoline would help a smoldering pile of leaves. After she had doused them, she took the gas can to the garage and returned in the still air to light a match. The gas fumes had spread and lay low on the lawn. Her match ignited a fireball that hurled her against a tree so hard she broke a sizeable branch. Wearing shorts, her legs were burned in almost the same configuration as mine. She was able to call her son who drove her to the hospital and then a few days later they transferred her to Dr. Terry's care.

When I rolled into the room, Mary was sitting, short and chunky, on the edge of an exam table. She was wearing shorts; she had advanced beyond her bandages and her compression garments. Her legs looked tan and smooth. I could see the paper towel texture of the grafting, but there was color and no malformation. When I learned that indeed her legs had received third-degree burns and looked this good now, I started to choke up and said, "You have the most beautiful legs I've ever seen!" She was thrilled and said she couldn't wait to go home and tell her husband!

I was filled with hope. Mary said the compression garments indeed hurt and caused many ingrown toenails but that they were so worth it. I thought that if that constant pressure on my healing skin would produce her result, I would tolerate the pain. (What no one told me was that my burns were significantly deeper than Mary's and there was no way that level of normalcy would ever be achieved.)

My healing continued to the point that my fingernails finally grew completely out and all the charring was gone from the nail bed. My face still had little pigment and never would have. Now ultra-violet light from the sun would cause immediate sunburn on the new, baby-like skin.

My legs still wouldn't stop barking, but at least now I had a control of the pain. I likened my hours of being awake to going to the amusement park. Each morning I was given the same number (I visualized 100) of "Energy Tickets" and "Pain Points." I started out each day with two imaginary buckets. One was filled and eventually would be emptied. The other was empty, waiting to be filled.

Depending on which rides (activities of daily life) I wanted to take, the "Energy Tickets" would be removed from the bucket at varying frequency. I could either have a really wild and fast ride and use some quickly or I could slowly spend them for a longer visit. Every hour I had my legs in a dependent position (down), I was adding pain points into the bucket.

When I depleted my energy tickets, there were no more. I had to crash. When my pain points had piled up in the once-empty bucket to the point they reached the brim, I couldn't carry any more pain. I had to give in to it. Morphine helped. Anything less was like sucking an ice cube. By day's end, I was completely spent and often ended up crying, the pain was so bad. The more depleted of energy I became, the higher the pain levels. There was good cause to just quit trying. Sitting, for the rest of my life sounded like the only recourse. I refused.

Energy conservation was of paramount importance to healing. Dr. Terry prescribed Remeron to bring me restorative sleep. What he didn't tell me was that it was also an appetite stimulant. After taking it at 9 p.m., I would be ravenous by 10 p.m. and start eating everything I could find. Before the drug put me down, it was not unusual for me to eat an entire bunch of celery laden with peanut butter and then dig in the jar with my fingers to scrape the bottom. And I don't even like peanut butter. I would talk in gibberish and argue with Barbie as she tried to pry the jar out of my sleepy grasp. What with the constant sitting and the newfound appetite late at night, I quickly regained the 30 pounds I lost and added 50 more. I would fall asleep with peanut butter smeared all over the sheets, pillow and my face. I was a mess.

I learned about the role that energy plays in our body's function as Barbie and I finally thought we would give intimacy a try again. Of all the emotions that were out of balance, physical longing wasn't even on the radar and we both missed it. During the hospitalization I had very few feelings – fear, fatigue, hunger, libido. I was so sedated with painkillers that I just existed.

I've included and then deleted, this experience into and out of my story several times as I try to examine how transparent, *Burned But Not Broken*, needs to be, but as I re-evaluate my goals of writing, it is to help the next guy, the next couple, just starting their lap of the catastrophic recovery race. Full disclosure is the best way to really help.

My buddy Bill Oades and I have always had a comfortable level of conversation about sex. We appreciated the fact that we were married to women that loved us more than we deserved. For the four of us to talk, tease, or both about the physical expression of love was an easy topic. I learned later that one of the first concerns for most of my guy friends was how I would recover in that department, but they were too shy to ask. Not Bill.

In one of the earliest conversations with him that I can remember, I think by phone, he asked me in hushed tones, "Mike, I know you've been to the bonfire of bonfires. I know the fire went up your legs. I've just got to know...if it roasted your wiener."

Even in my stupor I comprehended the question, but not knowing the answer, lifted the sheet to take a look and replied, "No, I think I'm good."

The "good" was from an exterior vantage point; what I didn't know was how the plumbing was being affected as many veins had been burned away and new routing was being formed for the blood supply to reach all extremities. All extremities.

Due to still being in leg splints and not able to move much, our rendezvous of romance was at best going to be more experimental than passionate. We were both relieved to see that the venous system had repaired itself sufficiently.

Things followed a normal course and conclusion with the exception that there was no evidence that indeed all was well.

Alarmed, puzzled, and scared that it was permanent, I asked the medical staff to clear the room on my next visit to Dr. Terry. I explained in unembarrassed terms what had happened and he calmly explained that he was pleased and relieved that full sensation had been restored for me. That was a surprise considering the depth of my burns. Secondly, he enlightened me that the production of semen was a very energy-depleting project for the male body.

The body would first use energy for life preservation. He explained that while semen was life giving, it was not life preserving. Preservation came before production. I was blown away by the clarity of the word picture. He assured me that when the body was convinced that I wasn't going to die, it would start letting up on the troops and rotate their work schedules. In their off days, they would put in some volunteer hours in the semen department. He was (as always), right.

I appreciated their efforts.

The road to healing was going to be a long one. Though my progress had snowballed, the end result would take four years. Knowing that made the pain more bearable as I often got discouraged with my limitations.

I was scooting up and down the steps now like a toddler on my backside and had walkers waiting at both ends of the staircase. I was brushing my own teeth and could sit in the shower. I had been deafened in my left ear by the explosion and hearing was not only difficult, but lots of voices at once were unnerving. I treasured the quiet.

I could not make my hands touch my legs. I would watch Barbie apply the salve and medicine. Or, if I did touch my legs, I turned my head. I just could not accept the connection that those healthy arms and malformed legs were a part of the same body. Some days I would lie in bed and just watch my legs spasm in pain. Searing bolts of pain would shoot through them as they jumped off the sheets. I tried to visualize that perhaps that was the ends of two nerves reconnecting like a live electrical wire. I hoped that the pain equaled gain.

Pain in itself was a personality manipulator. I had escaped pain all my life.

I had never had a broken bone or stitches. I had never been hospitalized. Now I was making up for those bonus years in spades.

Another purpose in writing this book is to explain to families of chronic pain sufferers how difficult it is for the patient to put on their game face on command. Perhaps much has been written about it, but until one has lived with it 24/7, it's impossible to describe how dominant pain can be. I felt like pain made me become someone I had never met. And I'm sure, at times, my family wished they hadn't met me either.

I learned the importance of not toughing it out, and the intelligence of staying ahead of the pain. I took the pain medicine, without fear of addiction, on schedule regardless of my pain levels. Eventually Dr. Terry would suggest alternate pain relief therapies that would allow me to use less and less opiate derivative. I eventually found some relief with acupuncture, which allowed me to stop wearing the compression tights. After two years, they had become my security blanket. They not only obscured the view of my scarred skin, but my legs started to feel better when softly compressed. Weaning burn victims off their compression garment, I learned, is often difficult. I had graduated out of my glove, but still had the tights and the separate booties that were custom made for my swollen, now size 14 feet. They were closed with a zipper on the ankle much like a ski boot.

Pain relief sometimes took both patience and distraction. In the past I had viewed those celebrities that were addicted to prescription painkillers as weaklings and lazy. Now walking in their shoes, metaphorically, I could see how easy it would be to give in to the pain and just pop another pill. Maybe 15 minutes early today...30 minutes earlier next week...and soon you're dependent. I was very blessed to have a family that would help me get flat and legs up as quickly as possible and as I started using over-the-counter pain reliever more and more, I would take the maximum dose and then distract my head with watching mindless television as my legs rested on a massaging inclined electric platform. I had learned from Dr. Terry that this combination of stimulation filled the passageways to my brain with the sensation of tingling, which blocked out the chance for pain to register in my thinking. In a sense I was distracting my body as well.

I also advised my family to just give me some space and I apologized frequently for my crabbiness. Barbie could often tell when I was in need of a pain reliever as my moods became dark and my words sharp.

As fatigue would settle in, I also had to listen to my body. For the first time, I couldn't push the machine of my body to do anything. Rather than sputtering out of gas, the cord had been yanked out of the wall. Many evenings I would be so exhausted from trying for a full day that my sternum ached. I learned the meaning of the word "bone tired." When I got to that point, there was nothing but rest that would reverse it.

As seesaw as my healing appeared, the best advice came from Paul Linneman – again. He told me not to measure my progress in weeks as that would become discouraging, but rather in months. That led to a journal of how I spent my days and I could see the improvement from month to month. Now I measure my improvement from season to season and then I lump the seasons together to compare it from year to year. I know there will come a time of diminishing return, but I haven't found it yet and when I do, I'll redefine the word "improvement."

I am not going to give in or give up.

NINE
"It's Only Going to Get Worse"

"Michael, this is Tommy Fagen. I'm calling to tell you that if you think it's bad now, it's only going to get worse."

As autumn deepened, so did my depression.

I had the privilege of getting acquainted with Tommy Fagen and Carla Pearman when I coordinated a fabulous wedding for them in October 2002. Tommy had waited for the right girl for 45 years and Carla, a successful ob/gyn, wasn't shopping for a mate when they fell in love.

Tommy's candor to many may seem so candid as to be disarming, but I quickly assessed him to be an authentic guy who was as real as dirt.

Tommy and Carla happened into my store on a busy Saturday to peruse tuxedo options. In helping them, it came to light that they had neither date nor venue. No plans were in place and they were putting the "tux horse" way before the cart. Ironically I had coordinated the wedding of Tommy's nephew but he never thought of hiring a coordinator for his own. He just thought by choosing a tuxedo, all the other details would fall into place.

We instantly liked each other and the pasture of the farm that Carla owns became a city of tents as 500 guests came to celebrate not just a marriage, but life.

Tommy had just recently recovered from his own near-death experience after he developed a build up of Vitamin A in his brain, causing stroke-like consequences. He was on a ventilator for many weeks and anointed for the Last Rites. His family of 10 siblings and loving parents kept vigil by his bedside as they watched the guy who had been the life of the party for years reduced to non-functional. Carla, his girlfriend only, was the one who the family relied on to help them navigate the uncharted waters of this rare ICU experience.

With the help of multiple brain surgeries and the installation of a shunt under his skull, Tommy, at age 43, came back to life. His motor function was so impaired that he had to re-learn to read, walk, and feed himself. His rehab was always a work in progress. Though he had trouble with short-term memory still, the one thing he didn't forget was what it felt like to be young and disabled.

Once he was on his feet, literally, he proposed to Carla who eagerly accepted as she wanted to be considered "next of kin" in case something would happen in his future, and she loved this crazy guy. The wedding was really a party of tremendous celebration on many levels – relief, joy, looking forward, new beginnings. Autumn colors in linens and flowers and fireworks reflected in the moonlit pond, celebrated their designation as "Mr. and Mrs." I was honored to be a part of such an emotional day.

Tommy stayed connected to me (as he does to everyone that ever comes into his life) but sensitive to our privacy during the first weeks, he didn't come to the hospital. They knew that there would be ample opportunities to help out once I was home and they were there.

The Nolte family developed a new cadence as Barbie went to work each morning after getting our three daughters off to school. I was so drugged that I slept the latest and awoke to an empty house. Upon awakening I would sometimes forget what had happened, as I had been horizontal for several hours. If I had needed morphine the night before, the early mornings were moments of exhilaration. I couldn't feel my legs! It was euphoria. The pain was gone, the blood not stinging through my veins and I felt like my old self again.

Once I sat upright on the edge of my bed collecting my balance and gripping my walker, the pain returned. I could see my changed reflection in the mirror. Hello reality.

Three mornings a week I had rehab at St. Joseph Hospital, just 15 minutes away. Jason, my physical therapist, would put me through the paces of lunges and upper body resistance training to build up my stamina. Some days I would have paraffin treatment on my burned hand, which was a big help in relieving the stiffness in the finger joints. With the exception of those opportunities, there was really no reason for me to leave the house. My days were spent simply sinking into couches and "the well." Life for my family had become routine and the man of the house was disabled.

Our breakfast room is flooded with morning light and is one of my favorite rooms. There I would read the paper and the thoughtful cards that were still arriving. There I would stare at the squirrels at the birdfeeder. There I would sit and watch it snow. There I would pray the rosary. There I sat when Tommy called.

His words were quick and to the point. He wasn't calling with dire predictions. He was calling with a plan.

"Now that you've been home awhile, people are going to go back to their lives. They are going to forget about you. As it gets colder, it's going to be harder to get you out. It's going to be harder for people to want to come see you. Even if you don't know it, you're suffering from depression. And it's going to get worse."

I couldn't wait.

"Here's the deal. I remember how it was for me when just walking around the block was a treat. To get fresh air made a huge difference in my day. I'm coming to get your ass out of your house once a week regardless if you want to do it or not. We're going to lunch in a place you've never been and we're going to a movie. Your vote doesn't count. I'm coming to get you."

And he did.

Week after week, Tommy came to get me out of the house. We explored the most out-of-the-way lunch spots that always required a long drive time. In those drives we shared life stories and discovered we were both storytellers. I loved talking to him. Oddly, I loved hearing him talk. His was a rich and interesting life and our values were much the same. He was one of the most interesting people I've ever met and it was literally fun to have a new friend. What seemed like "Tuesdays with Morrie," became our "Thursdays with Michael."

During this time of rehabilitation, I talked frequently by phone to my mother's sisters, my aunts Clara and Ethel, "The California Aunts." The distance that separated us geographically was never a distance of the heart and their children were some of my favorite maternal cousins.

Aunt Clara told me that as she entered her eighth year of lung cancer battle, she hoped she lived long enough to see me again before she died. I was alarmed that she even spoke of mortality. From Aunt Ethel, I learned that she and her daughter Carol were planning a trip to see Aunt Clara in the next month. I rallied myself out of "myself" and realized that this might be an important wish to grant. In going to see Aunts Clara and Ethel, the pleasure of such a wish would be mine.

It took buying two seats facing one another to transport my legs in one and hind quarters in another to fly there, but I did it. One of my lawyers flew with me and sure enough at the LAX airport, there was the long lens photographer clicking away to see, I assume, if I really needed the waiting wheelchair and airport attendant. (No worries, there wasn't going to be any surfing once I was on the West Coast.)

The surprise of my cousins Ed and Carol setting their mothers up for my appearance was a project they played out to the hilt. As "the girls" – ages 80 and 87 – relaxed before dinner at Ed's house in Camirrio, they were told that someone had stopped by to join them for the meal. I walked onto the patio with the sun behind me. Their initial reaction was "That neighbor looks a lot like our nephew Mike. But that's impossible." When I said, "Guess who's coming for dinner?" the look on their faces, fortunately captured on film... was priceless.

Over the next few days, they never stopped holding my good hand and saying repeatedly, "Oh honeeeeeey, I can't believe you're here." It was a visit I'll cherish for the rest of my life and one of the best expenditures of "Energy Points" I've ever invested.

Aunt Clara died nine days after I returned home. Aunt Ethel died 79 days later.

I had captured their biographies on video a few years earlier and was able to prepare for Aunt Clara a tribute video shown at her funeral and for Aunt Ethel a tribute booklet that contained both photos and her life story.

Sadness surrounded me.

My 48th birthday was quietly celebrated December 9. I was so grateful to have a birthday but was increasingly feeling unworthy to be alive.

The prosecution for the man who caused the wreck was set for December 11. The prosecuting attorney for Lafayette County (in which the wreck happened) called me to inquire as to what kind of punishment I felt appropriate for Paul Daniel. I was categorized one of the three victims – the State of Missouri, the Newton family, and the Nolte family.

Never having been in this role before, I didn't understand the definition of plea bargain agreement. I learned that it was a list of consequences that the perpetrator knew in advance as opposed to casting his fate before the court. There was no buffet line here from which to choose different entrees. The perpetrator had to agree to the entire list.

I listened to what the others had asked for – jail time, community service, maintaining the memorial site, carrying a photo of Officer Newton in his wallet, writing a letter of apology, etc.

I had really never thought of who had started this sequence of tragedy. I knew that Mike's death and my injuries were caused by a faulty fuel tank on a vehicle that had a long history of blowing up and killing people. The fact that the car was impacted didn't deliver either of us even a single broken bone. A gasoline-fed fire burned Mike to death and caused my suffering.

But the State of Missouri had a penal system that needed to be honored as well. As that man came into my conscious thought, I couldn't imagine him and asked for a description. Six-foot, six inches, 350 pounds. Big man.

This big man sitting in jail for even one day didn't change the outcome. Mike was still dead and I was still in non-stop pain. After two days of contemplation as to what I really wanted or needed, I decided I wanted just one hour of the man's time and that's all I asked of the court. One hour, private room, man to man, no lawyers to speak for us, no wives to comfort us, no media to record us. Just him and me.

It was the first thing he refused.

The plea bargain option was tossed out and he was going to court. December 11 would be a tough day, my lawyers said. "Bring some friends."

That morning our group of support arrived at the Civil War era courthouse glimmering in its white-pillared formality on a lawn of new snow. Streams of uniformed troopers were headed in the front door. My stomach tightened. I had no idea what was ahead. Thankfully my friend Steve Heeney had driven us and Barbie had Marie Adrian with her for support. Eleven other friends waited inside.

As we walked in from the blinding sunlight, the dim hallway came into focus as news camera lights illuminated our entrance and our lawyers greeted us. I was escorted to the front row. It was standing room only as troopers, reporters and friends crowded in. I had previously asked if my lawyers could arrange a private meeting with Mrs. Newton prior to this coming together and both sides advised against it. I complied, but wish I hadn't.

When Shonnie Newton was escorted to the front row across the aisle, our gaze met only momentarily. She instantly retreated in sobs back into the corridor. Inside the courtroom, we sat there with our own tears listening to her sorrow.

Upon her return, I didn't dare look up again. Neither of us could take it. Then they brought in Paul Daniel.

It was the first time for all of us to see the monster. There had been no photos of him in all the press to date. After being examined for injuries that horrible morning, his mother-in-law picked him up and drove him home. Now there he was. There had been a person, not just fate, karma, bad luck, or evil force behind all this.

As Judge Frerking opened the hearing, we listened to testimony from the dispatcher who received and made the emergency calls, the first trooper on the scene, the audio tape of the 911 calls and saw on a screen the view from the camera on the responding trooper's dashboard. The blazing Crown Victoria was almost unseen in the thick black smoke. It had indeed been an inferno.

When it was time for Shonnie to approach the bench and read her Victim's Impact Statement, she was nearly inaudible. She appeared tiny, devastated and alone. My heart broke for her. What she had seen and suffered was unimaginable.

My turn followed. The Victim's Impact Statement was the prepared answers to the questions: What happened? How where you injured? What punishment do you seek?

In preparing my answers at home I recalled the book *Black Like Me* in which a man chose to dye his skin and to suffer the prejudice that comes toward African Americans simply because of color. I was always puzzled as to why someone would put himself in the path of harm.

I wrote of that analogy, but my lawyers thought it too wordy and irrelevant, thus edited out the book's reference. That ended up causing months of hard feelings from some of the troopers toward me.

After I was sworn in, it took me several minutes to just get myself under control and begin speaking. I started to explain what happened on May 22, by now saying, "Through no fault of my own, forty percent of my body suffered third-degree burns." All the troopers heard were the first six words. Some of them thought I was defiant and disrespectful in my attitude. To this day, that line of thinking still puzzles me.

At the end of the testimonies, a tribute video of Mike's life was shown. It had been created for his funeral and provided images of his childhood, growing up, marrying, and most importantly his identity as a trooper. The cliché expression of "not a dry eye in the house" was certainly apt here and there shouldn't have been.

Paul Daniel then stood to address the court, which was basically talking to Shonnie and me. I thought that even though the guy had denied my request to talk to him, I would give him the respect of direct eye contact. I just looked at him as he stood in the center of the room. He was obviously the object of hatred for the troopers who had gathered, wanting a pound of his flesh. The hulking form, with a bad hair cut on top of no neck, stood there wringing his hands and said he wished he could start May 22 over, but he couldn't. He was really upset with what had happened. I just returned his gaze, with no expression. He never apologized.

To end his soliloquy he then turned the dagger with the twist of, "Hope you remember it was just an accident and accidents can happen to anybody." I nearly jumped to strangle him! This had been no accident! Who in their right mind drives the interstate highway with their leg propped on the dashboard? Who reaches completely below eye level to retrieve their sunglasses when they're speeding at 65 mph? This had been no accident!

I was overwhelmed by the entire gut-wrenching ordeal. The troopers filed out and formed an honor guard along the hallway as we recessed. We left in the glare of bright press lights and returned in silence to our car parked on the snowy street just where we had left it, as if none of that had just happened.

The hour drive back was the last time I talked to friends for several days. Once home, I literally pulled the covers over my head and stayed there the rest of the day. The phone rang non-stop as news coverage started playing of the morning's events. None of the calls were answered.

Paul Daniel had been charged with four misdemeanors – failure to drive in a single lane; careless and imprudent driving; failure to yield to an emergency vehicle, and failure to drive a commercial vehicle without a chauffeur's license. He had received a light sentence of six months in jail. It was more than our lawyers wanted. It wasn't enough for the troopers. I didn't care. I had just seen the boogey man. I had just seen the flesh and blood family of the man who died sitting beside me. All the characters in this tragic play now had faces, not just roles.

This piece of the journey triggered the beginning of a malaise that I couldn't shake. Day after day I replayed, in my mind, the video of a happy man and his family. We had been subjected to the same exact catastrophe and yet he was taken and I was spared. Why? Why? Why?

After the World Trade Center murders, I heard the term "survivor's guilt" used a lot. I didn't understand it. These people should have been thankful that they were not harmed...I hadn't been in their shoes.

Now I was and now I understood perfectly the emotions – the unexplainable, impossible to define, depression that sits on the shoulders of the survivors. In my case there was no support group. I was the sole survivor of a catastrophic car explosion.

In my case, the beginning of survivor's guilt was as specific as a single moment of a single day. It began the morning of December 11, 2003, at the Lafayette County Courthouse in Lexington, Missouri. I let it go months later on a spring morning at Mile Marker 47 a year after the wreck. Or so I thought.

Throughout those weeks following that day in court, I was paralyzed with depression. I would spend day after day sitting by the fireplace weeping at the injustice that Mike was dead and I was alive. I recalled the daily question of the psychiatrist, "Do you feel guilty for being alive?" The answer now was a resounding "Yes."

I called a meeting with my legal team, Davis, Bethune and Jones and we spent the afternoon in their offices on the top floor of City Center Square overlooking all of downtown Kansas City and the Missouri river. The view could not have been more exhilarating as snowflakes swept past the full glass walls.

Inside, my chest was hollow, my voice heavy, my eyes non-stop spigots of tears as I told them I wanted to halt the civil trial preparation. I didn't feel worthy to receive the expected monetary award from Ford Motor Company as it was held accountable for the havoc it wreaked in two families. One family had no husband, father and son. My family still had me. A diminished me, but still me. That had to be enough.

These "Three Wise Men" as I called them – Grant Davis, Scott Bethune, and Tom Jones – listened with genuine concern and when I was done, they asked if I would consider another viewpoint.

They felt that by combining my case with Shonnie's, it enhanced her case and if I really wanted to help her receive financial compensation, I shouldn't walk out of that role.

Furthermore, Scott pointed out the lop-sidedness of auto-makers that placed profit before human suffering and felt like this was a landmark case that could possibly make Ford finally listen and fix the car that had killed and maimed so many. The Ford Pinto had had a similar pattern and finally they stopped making it. I was one of only a handful of survivors of the Crown Victoria fatal history and I had the capacity to tell the story.

The money aside, though I felt my family did deserve it, the thought of ensuring this tragedy could stop with me, was enough to keep me in the lawsuit. I acquiesced, as I've never been one to run from a fight, but I was really going to need the support of this firm to keep me strong enough to do battle with Goliath. Could I really make a difference for motorists throughout the country? Maybe. The lawyers located for me a skilled psychiatrist in St. Louis, Dr. Wayne Stillings, who they felt would be helpful in treating my post-traumatic stress disorder and the survivor's guilt. They were right.

Dr. Stillings had extensive training in the burn unit before he specialized in psychiatry. In talking with him, he knew the terminology, and he understood the terrors of the tank. He could finish my sentences when I broke into tears when I told him how unworthy I felt in still being alive. He asked to examine my injury and when I de-panted, he was the first person to acknowledge what I knew, "You have been terribly burned and your body will never be the same again. The pain must be incredible."

"Yes to all the above."

He continued with, "To have fought this hard, to come this far, you are not unworthy...but lucky to be alive." His words planted a seed in my psyche.

The flight home from St. Louis was the first time I had prayed in a long time. It was a prayer of supplication to discern my new purpose. If I was alive, "Why was I spared? For what was I spared?"

The answer came shortly thereafter.

Tommy provided temporary relief from my housebound apathy, but there were still empty hours in an empty house. I won't say there was a day of hitting the bottom but rather a day of "bouncing back."

I had spent months reflecting what had happened. Looking back. Counting the weeks since. There was no thought of what could happen. There was no thought of my future, only my past.

I decided that whining was unproductive. All my life, I had been a producer. I was the guy who longed for that 25th hour so I could accomplish more. Michael Nolte was alive and by damn he better do something with these days he had been given.

Not surprisingly, once this light bulb went on, I called a strategic planning meeting with my brain and my body. For 48 years, my brain could tell my body to push a little harder, to get a little more done. Now my body was giving the orders and it was winning over my brain. Enough.

Just because I couldn't do everything I had done before the wreck didn't mean I could nothing at all. I vowed to start this 180-degree turnaround by thinking of two Gestures of Service I could provide each day. One for my family. One for someone outside my family. By God (and for God), I was going to lift someone else up, like prayers had lifted me up during the long ICU stay.

Enter the toaster.

Still on the counter was the toaster, left from Caroline's breakfast in all its smeary, baked-on grunge glory. This once shiny chrome appliance, usually stored out of sight, was long overdue for cleaning. It was gritty and dirty. The toaster was my target.

Tucking it under my arm, I made my way back to the table using my walker and covered my lap with a bath towel. Working with only one good hand, it took an hour and a half to wrestle it clean.

But I did it!!

Then I remembered a friend who I knew had a chemo treatment that morning. I called her and told her that I was praying for her and then ripped off a decade of the rosary.

I did it.

Two acts of service to others. And during that time, I was too busy to ruminate about myself. The whining had stopped.

I had been of service to others, and, in the time spent thinking of others, I did not focus on my own troubles. I felt encouraged and reaffirmed that God has a purpose for each of our lives, and regardless of how insignificant we feel our contributions may be, it honors Him and others when we realize as much.

Our toaster would become my symbol of recovery. When life isn't as planned, I offer that reminder. Find a way each day, however simple, to lift up others with the day that you have been given. It could be something as simple as cleaning a toaster.

Each day after, I started with a plan. Sometimes the Gestures of Service were on a to-do list by my bed. Pretty soon I had pages of things I could accomplish, people I could help.

Over the course of time, I organized 34 years worth of photographs in annual albums and wrote on the back of each one. I was so proud of that project, I left them arranged on their spines across the hearth room floor for almost six months, the labels clearly marked. A small triumph and an appreciated gesture by my family.

Then I started to write a book, "The History of the Nolte Family in America." I had wanted to do this for years and never made the time. Now I had it. I completed the research, interviewed by phone relatives all over the country, collected the old pictures, reprinted obituaries, and wrote a 56-page narrative of eight generations of my family and their passage from Germany. I designed the family tree down to the newest babies. I had the charts laminated for use as placemats, so kids could easily trace their place in the lineage. Another triumph and another gesture.

In a moment of temporary insanity, I ordered new sliding baskets for the cabinets and in one day completely re-organized the kitchen as a surprise for Barbie. The pantry was affixed with labels and all the cookware in its new better suited home. Big mistake. No triumph. No appreciation.

(Note to self and others: Guys, stay out of your wife's kitchen unless you're helping – with her consent.)

I tempered my pain, better managed my days, and started to understand that I had been given not a second chance, but a second life. As I reversed the hourglass, I visualized a toolbox that God filled before we were ever born. It was ready to accompany us to earth where He asked us to use these tools in a way no one else possibly can. He had prepared me, spared me, and now was renewing the lease on me. I was still a renter on His real estate and I was beginning to understand, finally, the purpose of my life, my place in the world.

TEN
Giving Credit Where Credit Is Due

The "S.S. Nolte's Bridal" was taking on water but still afloat during the 15 months it sailed without her captain. The door kept swinging largely due to reputation, and many new brides didn't know or didn't care that I wasn't at the helm. My first mate, Barbie, had insisted that the flag stay at full mast.

I always looked forward to my return trips to the Burn Clinic as they were usually going to leave me with a sense of progression. They were exhausting but gave Barbie and me a welcomed four hours alone as she drove and I lay in back of the van with my head between the seats talking with her.

In one of those early trips, we finally had the chance to think and I broached the topic of the business. I felt it was unfair to expect her to step into my shoes when she had 20 years of nursing experience to fall back on.

"If you want to sell it, downsize or close it, I'll be okay with your decision," I told her.

She replied, "The business is yours. You founded it. You've made it what it is. I'm not going to make the decision of its future without you. I plan to keep it running until you can come back and decide on its future based on your recovery."

I was amazed, inspired, grateful, and awed. I knew what that was going to take. (I knew what that took without a disabled spouse at home.) I didn't know how anybody could be in charge of two such enormous projects. I don't think I could have done it.

Barbie had to clean house when she learned of employees sharing with clients their personal doubts as to the future viability of the company. With her new team in place, she modeled dedication to doing the best she could with what she had.

Fortunately for the Nolte family someone had our back. That "someone" was Northwestern Mutual Financial Network.

In the early 90s, my neighbor Gary Meyerpeter, a bank vice president and a "money guy," recommended me to his insurance agent Pete Graff of the Columbia, Missouri, office. Not knowing jack about disability insurance but realizing that I had no Plan B, I believed the pitch and signed on.

Through the years not only did a friendship develop, but I trusted the company. I trusted the Moody's ratings of "Aaa", and Standard & Poor's "AAA," year after year. Not only was I being covered for disaster, but I was also actually saving money. The automatic debit was painless and the peace of mind enormous. I could put my energy into growing my business and know that my family was provided for in the event of my disability. (But of course that would never happen to me.)

Over a decade of annual reviews with Pete, we had tweaked my coverage so many times I couldn't remember what I had added and dropped (as cash flow directed.) I knew if I died, there was a chunk for Barbie and literally registered that reassurance as I felt myself dying on the helicopter. To this day, I can't believe that really happened; that it really entered my mind. But it did. I have since wondered how I would have felt in that instant, if I had not had the life insurance in place? I doubt that I would have said, "Too bad for them." I think I would have entered the gates of heaven tormented.

What I couldn't remember was the amount of my disability insurance coverage. It didn't take Pete Graff more than 24 hours to see the news of the wreck on television that he was in the waiting room talking to Barbie. He explained that we had to wait 90 days to qualify, but then Northwestern Mutual would kick in to help us. And they did and still are.

Not only were my life insurance premiums waived, but every month a check came that covered the essentials of our family's needs. If Barbie never brought home a dollar from the business, we could have made it, thanks to Northwestern.

In the ensuing months I came to understand the vital role that good insurance should play in our lives. My friends warned us of the mountains of paperwork, the endless phone calls to substantiate claims and the reluctance to pay out that they had had with their insurers. We never had any of that.

With a single fax and an authorization from Dr. Terry, the benefit checks were cut. There were some months Barbie didn't get the fax sent by deadline and my claims representative, Tricia Hosley, would call from the home office in Milwaukee and remind her. There were some months Dr. Terry was late with his part and Northwestern sent the check anyway.

After I returned to work part-time, Northwestern sent Ray Wilson from Texas to qualify my disability. My attorneys prepared me, "This is the guy who's coming to turn off the faucet." The suggested one-hour visit turned to three and when he saw my legs, he simply quietly said, "Mr. Nolte, Northwestern Mutual will always be there for you."

There was a rehabilitation consultant, Gwen Stinebrink, who interviewed me by phone as to the possibility of future vocational training that could provide some replacement income. It had been suggested by friends that I might consider training as a professional speaker. I had a B.S. in Speech Communication and now had a story to share that might help people. I felt that maybe that was a tool in my toolbox that deserved exploring.

The application for vocational re-training with a speaker's bureau though seemed to need specific answers as to the exact classes, the anticipated salary, etc. I had none of those answers and threw away the application for tuition help. After several months, Gwen called to see why I hadn't submitted the forms. I explained my assumption that I wouldn't qualify and we visited for more than an hour about my plans for my future. The week before Christmas she sent me a check that covered 70 percent of the tuition with a personal note of encouragement and holiday wishes. I nearly fell over.

Does Northwestern Mutual pay me a nickel to add this into my book? Absolutely not. In fact they don't even know I'm writing this, but I have always believed in giving credit where it's due and when the client care has been what I've experienced (and I've since learned this is the norm for all their policy holders), I'll gladly share the news.

As I tried to visualize returning to work, I drove to my store after hours and spent an evening alone in my office. I sat in my chair, looked through the files and recognized none of the bride's names. There was new inventory, new window displays, and new advertising strategies. I realized that it had moved ahead without me. I wondered if I still had a place. I wondered if I had game.

It was another of the many emotional crossroad experiences.

I embraced the concept of re-entry and hosted a Back to Work Party at the store August 11, 2004. Nearly every one of the 100 or so guests accepted the "He's baaaaack" lime and purple invitation. Caterers, florists, musicians all gave their product or services as a gift to the celebration. A national bridal magazine carried pictures of the party. The highlight of the evening was Barbie's toast and presentation of a satin pillow that held the key to the front door!

The first weeks back were composed of two- or three-hour shifts that would require a full recuperation day to follow. Just the energy required to be dressed and "on" was exhausting.

As the schedule grew more tolerable, the trips to the burn clinic were spaced further and further apart. But the visits with my lawyers increased in frequency as we prepared for the civil trial that opened May 16, 2005. (Just a week short of the two-year mark they had predicted.)

The build-up for the trial required depositions from each of us and interviews with several friends regarded as "lay witnesses." These were people who knew me before, during, and after the wreck experience and could speak to how it had affected me. The media speculation was intense as lots of Kansas Citians were aware of a similar trial that concluded six weeks earlier in East St. Louis for the Jablonskis.

Mr. and Mrs. Jablonski were rear-ended near the time of my wreck as they were stopped in a construction zone. The typical fiery explosion resulted in Mr. Jablonski's death and his wife's painful hospitalization and transfer to a nursing home. They had been married 50 years. The jury was enraged to learn that Ford had planned to redesign the dangerous tank for their Crown Victorias purchased by law enforcement agencies, but had no plans to do so for civilians. The Jablonskis were awarded $43 million dollars from Ford.

For the troopers it was a razor edge to walk. Did they wish the best for the widow of their fallen brother? Or were they to remain silent about the vehicles that they were required to ride in everyday?

The anticipation culminated as we learned that Barbie and my parents would be required to be in the courtroom every day and the trial would last five weeks. Our daughter Emma-Lea would graduate from high school one of those days and Barbie couldn't be there. Our Silver Anniversary was May 24, and we couldn't have a celebration, Barbie had to be in the courtroom.

The rehearsals for our times on the witness stand were intense and nerve wracking. They caused me to dredge up memories I didn't want to think about. I knew I was going to be asked specific questions that demanded answers, under oath, about the last few minutes of Officer Newton's life. I was going to have to answer them in front of his parents and widow.

The J.D.R.F. Ball in Kansas City is always held the first Saturday in May. As a stress buster, our friends entreated us to join them for the black-tie ball, which is hosted by Juvenile Diabetes Research Foundation. We had attended this event with the same group many times. It was one of our favorite charity fundraisers. The ball was a week before the trial opened. It was May, the month of the wreck, and I was feeling waves of survivor's guilt.

As I saw my tuxedoed reflection, I felt a quaking in my chest. Something wasn't comfortable and it wasn't the tux.

In retrospect, there were "triggers."

Crowds still bothered me. Stimuli were hard to process. This was my debut back into a social setting, and lots of people seemed very glad to see us back after a two-year absence.

I just knew as soon as I walked into the ballroom I shouldn't be there.

"Mike, you don't look like you feel well," my friend Steve said just after we sat down at our table. "Do you need to go out and get some air?"

"No, I'm fine, Steve," I said.

Watching my face blanche, Steve knelt by my chair.

"Mike, I'm telling you, you really don't look right. Why don't we go outside for a while?"

"No, Steve, I think I'm going to be fine," I reiterated.

As the large screens explained the blessing of health without the handicap of diabetes, I could feel myself slipping down the well...rapidly.

I couldn't help but think of the unfairness that I was re-emerging back into my life, with my friends, with my wife, while Shonnie Newton would never have that privilege and her husband's charred corpse lay in the ground. It was survivor's guilt x 100. I thought about Tyler Newton, Mike's son. So alone.

I made my way from the ballroom through the crowd.

Once I got to the lobby, I leaned against a pillar for support.

"Come on. Let's get you out of here," Steve said.

I closed my eyes and, for the first time, I saw the inside of the car – the orange flames and Mike Newton's face – outlined in fire and melting.

"Steve, I shouldn't be alive. What happened to Mike Newton should have also happened to me." If I couldn't bring Mike back here, I could level the field by putting myself there.

Hotel security was quickly involved and 911 called.

"Get me a gun! Get me a gun!" I begged over and over.

I could feel the barrel of the gun in the roof of my mouth. It felt right. I jammed my fingers as far as I could into my mouth thinking that they were the barrel of Steve's deer rifle.

I was handcuffed and nearly carried to the police cruiser. When I saw the car to which I was being nearly carried, I balked. It was a Crown Victoria. The cops didn't care what my issues were; I was forced to get in as they kicked my knees from behind and shoved my head down and into the front seat.

I was allowed one call.

I had the presence of mind call Tom Jones, the lawyer I always said "drew the short straw" as it seemed his role to babysit the client. Tom arrived just after Steve and Phil came by taxi. A shot of Valium calmed me and talk therapy took me off the ledge. I couldn't stop crying, but finally I was allowed to return home.

The next day, the lawyers had me on a plane to see Dr. Stillings. I was losing it. He reassured me that he had expected a mental breakdown at some point and I was diagnosed with a "shredded psyche." It was more than the human brain can accept as reality or process. He gently helped me sort through the memories as to which were facts and which were nightmares. All of it stayed.

During my visit, Dr. Stillings explained the concept of "triggers" and gave me the coping mechanisms to stay strong enough to get through the trial. I would be called to testify and I had to be able to do it with composure to ensure that the jury heard the whole truth and nothing but the truth... so help me God.

I was only allowed in the courtroom one day. The day of my testimony,

I reported to the private witness room by way of back door. There I finally was allowed to meet Shonnie and Mike's mother, Bobbie, as they waited to be escorted into the courtroom. When I saw them, we simply embraced and shed more tears.(Surely we were in the last lap now.)

I was on the stand for more than two hours. The courtroom was packed. The reporting of my testimony was a quarter page article in the next day's newspaper. I was very embarrassed.

Through out the five weeks, e-mails and cards of encouragement flowed in every day. I had the new ones taped to the kitchen cabinets for Barbie and my parents, each evening. I maintained an online journal for the friends across the country that wanted to know how the trial was going.

The day of final arguments produced an overflowing gallery again. Barbie, my parents, and all three daughters were there for the reading of the verdict. The opinion of everyone who sat through the process was unanimous. The evidence was clear. There had been a history of this defect. There were no injuries caused by the impact. Micheal Newton and Michael Nolte had been burned but not broken.

The jury awarded Barbie $500,000, Shonnie $4 million, and me $4.5 million. They felt the negligence of the driver was something that shouldn't be overlooked, so they assigned the fault to his employer.

The trucking company, Tradewinds, had two employees, no cash and no assets. It is called a "non-recoverable verdict."

Ford paid nothing.

It appeared the most shocked person in the courtroom was Ford's lawyer. He admitted that he had the punitive damages specialist on a plane from Detroit to negotiate the remainder of what he anticipated to be additional damages.

The sense of loss was like a hammer to the head. My family simply sat in a stupor that afternoon. One of my lawyers, Grant Davis, the senior partner of the firm, came to be with us. It was almost like the worst funeral I've ever attended. (But I had already had that.)

Grant Davis made a prediction afterwards that, sadly, has come true.

"There will be more gasoline-fed fires," he said. "More troopers will die."

And they have.

The teaser for the evening news stated the misinformation of "Local business owner awarded millions of dollars and is still not happy." Thankfully Grant was there to hear that on television and after a few phone calls, that line of reporting was corrected. To people not familiar with the legal system, they didn't get it. "Awarded" and "Receiving" are two completely different realities.

Barbie urged me to be respectful of the press that had been so supportive for the previous two years and not hide now. What image did that portray? Thus I did agree to a press conference on our front porch in which I defined the difference between a tragedy and a trauma.

The Newtons had suffered a tragedy from which they would never recover. The Noltes would heal from their trauma. My worth was not measured by dollars in a bank but rather by the three daughters who stood beside me now. I thanked our city for its incredible support through this entire ordeal. And I thanked God that I was alive to participate in this press conference.

Barbie, my strong rock, my anchor, dissolved in my arms. She had been through so, so much. She wept, "I thought God was going to do the right thing this time." I replied, "Barbie, God did. Ford didn't."

"Shonnie doesn't have what you have right now. Your husband is here to hold you and we're going to get through this last part together."

And we did.

ELEVEN
Dave and Troy: Joy and Joy

Things had to be getting better. I had undergone an additional surgery for the repair of skin grafts that were lifting from the edges and some more work on my re-crafted ear. I was walking with just a cane now and in the house didn't use it at all. I was still needing to carry an umbrella to shield me from ultra-violet light, but I had gotten pretty good at applying the 90 SPF sun block and the special make-up for burn victims. Most people say they can't tell (thankfully).

I was out of the clunky healing boots and now wearing slightly less clunky special shoes that accommodated the prosthetic devices molded for the bottoms of my feet.

I got started on a low carb/high protein plan to shed the 50 pounds and investigated joining a gym. However in touring it, I just couldn't get comfortable with the contrast of my lower body swimming in a pool with buff guys in Speedos. I missed both the tan and the "buff."

With the trial over, the way was clear to finally, finally, finally learn the details of what happened that day. Until then I was kept in the dark so my testimony wasn't compromised with the suggestions that might be planted by an innocent comment made by anyone at the scene that day. I was to relate the truth as only I remembered it, not from what someone else told me happened.

I was given unlimited time and access to the files and tapes at Davis, Bethune and Jones. I watched with rapt attention the depositions of many witnesses that never made it to the stand. The EMTs, the Life Flight crew, the firemen, the troopers. Most of what they shared was indeed new news.

The tapes I didn't want to watch though were those marked: "David Bryan" and "Troy Brinkoetter." I wanted to see the real deal, not a video version.

In my head, I conjured up at least five great plans as to how I could organize this reunion. I fantasized even more about what I would buy for them with the Ford award as a gift of appreciation. I could just hear Bob Barker's voice, "A new car!" (obviously, not a Ford), a cruise, a new home. The sky was the limit. These guys had literally saved my life. How do you say "thank you" adequately? And then there was no Ford compensation.

The local media had all asked to be present when this reunion took place, and I wanted Dave and Troy to finally come out of hiding and be recognized for their heroism. But suddenly the national media started calling and wanted the story. My allegiance fell though to CBS for *The Early Show* as my friend Debbye Turner was a correspondent there. They even had a segment titled "American Hero." It was a perfect fit.

The CBS producer, Scott Fraser, organized the plan for a crew to be in Kansas City to re-create the day of the wreck and then do vignettes of a "day in the life of" Dave, Troy, and myself, all privately of course. Then after two weeks of editing, we were to be flown to New York and the piece would be aired. We would then be brought from three separate rooms and reunited on their set, live. Scott explained that they needed the controlled lighting and sound that only their studios could provide for such an important piece. I begrudgingly agreed.

The local media, to which I felt indebted for its support, was now kicked out of this plan. That was the last thing I wanted to do. It excluded so many people. I didn't want it that orchestrated. I didn't want to go to New York. I didn't know if that was comfortable for Dave and Troy and on and on. But I quickly learned that once you sign away the rights to your story, it is no longer your story but rather that of the network. My artistic control was nil.

The trial ended June 14. The CBS crew arrived July 19. Regardless of my opinion being considered, at least the waiting would be over. I was going to meet the Good Samaritans who were larger than life in my mind.

Barbie had seen Dave and Troy both on the stand. I had sent them each cards of gratitude, filtered and mailed through my lawyers, on the occasions of my birthday, Christmas, and the crash anniversary. I received a Christmas card from each of them – at least I saw their penmanship! It was like an adoptee searching for birth parents.

I knew in advance that after the crew was done filming at my house, we were headed to a private dining room at Yia Yia's, one of our favorite restaurants, for a thank you dinner. CBS had made all the arrangements.

Our living room became a sound studio. Phones, air-conditioning, toilets turned off. Even my neighbor was asked to postpone mowing his grass. Scott was very gracious and inclusive of his crew and introduced each of them to my family and me.

Debbye and I sat knee-to-knee as she began the interview. She shared that the interviews earlier with Dave and Troy had been very emotional and her connection to this story was more than just in the pursuit of good journalism. I knew I had made the right decision to go with CBS.

Her opening question was a benign; "It's been two years since I last saw you. How are you doing now?" and my eyes just started filling up. A million facets of these last 26 months flashed in my subconscious. What a struggle it had been. Now the journey was almost done. Debbye's fawn-like eyes teared up as well.

The producer yelled, "Cut."

Debbye explained that both Dave and Troy had eaten up lots of hours of union labor earlier in the day as they too had struggled to stay composed for their interviews. These crewmen were about to go into overtime and we had to get this wrapped up. I told her the only way I could talk about it, with her, was to look beyond her shoulder when I answered.

That's how we proceeded. Take two and then a wrap.

Finally, the interview was over. The lights came down. The sound equipment packed away. Surprisingly they decided to "just get a little footage" of the dinner and re-set up at Yia Yia's. I fell for it.

In the dining room filled with all round tables, we were seated at the only rectangular table, with me placed in the center of the table, my girls scattered in chairs and Debbye and Scott at opposite ends. The seats on either side of me were left vacant. I was facing the large window, "for better light spilling on the subject's face." I fell for it.

I thought about the poor conversational dynamics this seating arrangement posed and reflected that if I had been in charge, I would have had me seated at one end so I could talk with everyone much easier. But CBS was paying, so I wasn't saying. (What I realized later was that they needed my back to the door.)

After wine had been ordered and we truly started to relax, Scott casually mentioned, "Oh Mike, by the way, there's somebody that I wanted to meet you earlier, but he's just arrived.

Remembering how solicitous Scott had been to the crew, I thought it was another sound tech or someone late leaving the house. Just as I turned for a quick and casual handshake, Barbie (seated across from me and looking toward the open door) glanced over my head and said softly, "Oh my gosh."

Immediately, I knew something was of huge importance, but I couldn't even form a thought as I was turning to shake the "sound tech's," hand and he leaned down and said softly, "Mike...I'm Troy Brinkoetter."

The earth...absolutely...stopped...spinning...at that very moment.

I was so stunned that I could barely comprehend the words. I took his hand in my own...watched it...become the hand that had saved my life by pulling me out of a burning car.

I leaned over and kissed it. My forehead touched his backhand as sobs started welling into my throat. As I stood to embrace him, there was a man behind him. "I'm Dave Bryan."

It was truly, finally again, too much heaven. I was a goner.

All I could think to say to them was "For the rest of my life...thank you for the rest of my life."

Behind the men stood their wives, Julia Brinkoetter and Susan Bryan. My daughters sat like stone statues at the table watching in silence as this tableau played itself out. This was the very moment for which their father had waited for two years. These were the men that allowed them to still have a father.

Debbye breathed a sigh of relief when Scott indicated that they had indeed captured all the raw emotion that truly told this incredible saga. The lights and cameras eventually pulled away and Dave and Troy sat in the empty seats beside me. For the next two hours we didn't know what to say to each other. The conversation was stilted at best and Debbye, who felt now like she knew all of us, kept the conversation flowing. Throughout the meal, Dave or Troy was in physical contact with me the entire time.

At times I would well up, for no reason, and they would pat my leg, hold my hand, or rub the back of my head or shoulder. I think for them it was an overload as well, considering the last time they saw me in real life, my naked, burned body was being strapped to a gurney and hurried to a helicopter. They had watched some of the televised updates and read the news accounts, but never had seen me. I think they were as awed to see and touch the guy they had saved as I was to see and touch them. It was almost like I was the injured child and they wanted to be sure I was going to be okay this time. If there was a hurt, physical or emotional, they could take away, they would.

Knowing what a control freak I can be, the second we headed home in our car, Justine asked, "Dad are you mad at CBS for doing that?"

I answered her honestly, "That's exactly what I didn't want to have happen and it's exactly the best way it could have happened. No I'm not mad, I'm actually relieved. Now the wait is over."

When the feature ran August 2, Dave and Troy joined me for a press conference as we watched it together. The local media did get its time with us then and asked the guys lots of questions. About 50 other friends were in the ballroom as well and enjoyed the light brunch offered as a gift from the Ritz Charles – one of my favorite reception venues.

Afterwards, my heroes, their families, and I headed to my house for a private lunch. Finally we could talk, talk, talk and listen, listen, listen. The questions could be asked. Some answers will never be known.

What made you come to the passenger side first? I don't know.

Did you see me inside? No, too much smoke.

Who was there first? Dave. Troy appeared out of nowhere just as Dave was saying to himself when he lifted under my arm pit, "I can't do this by my..."

Did you ever see Officer Newton? No, Dave reached in and yelled, "Take my hand, take my hand." No response.

Did the driver's side glass ever break? No, Troy was swinging a fire - extinguisher at it like a bat and it wouldn't break.

What happened to the glass on my side? Don't know; it just wasn't there.

Was I heavy or tangled to pull out? No, it was like lifting a baby out of a crib. They did it in one fluid motion. At 189 pounds, they never felt my weight.

Did others who stopped, help? There were about 75 people that had already stopped and were standing at a distance watching the inferno. They did not come closer.

What did you do after you gave your report to the patrol? Dave returned to Kansas City and went to Susan's school to tell her he had a role in the wreck seen on the news in the teacher's lounge. She didn't believe him, as he didn't even smell like smoke. Troy went on to Columbia for a doctor's visit for the slight stroke he had suffered three days earlier. He required a wheelchair to get out of the car.

What did my lawyers tell you to do? Go home and don't talk about it to anyone. It might jeopardize the potential jury pool and they didn't want a change of venue request from Ford.

Did you want to come see me as bad as I wanted to meet you? They both had been in the parking garage of the hospital (on two separate trips) when my lawyers dissuaded them from making contact with my family as it could hurt the case.

I had some of the hospital photos available for them if they wanted to see them. Dave flipped through them three pages at a time. Troy looked at a couple and left the table. I saw him outside on the deck and thought he was smoking.

As I went out to give him some grief about cutting his own life short with such a habit, I realized he was crying. He turned to me and referencing the pictures asked, "I had no idea it was that bad. Mike, are you sure you're glad we saved you?!"

Understanding the basis for his question, I replied, "Honestly, not always. And at the time those pictures were taken, not at all. But now Troy, getting to meet you and Dave...absolutely."

As weird as it seems now, I had organized the conclusion of the day to include a session with my local psychologist, Dr. Phyllis Carrozzo. I gently invited the guys to go with me and told them she had been a great help in processing the post-traumatic stress syndrome. Both guys immediately said, "Yes."

In the session, Dr. Carrozzo could barely ask questions that didn't bring a flood of tears from one of them. I said very little as I realized that I had had a two year jump on coming to grips with this tragedy and Dave and Troy had had absolutely no professional help. They were just now starting their own mental health recovery.

I also acknowledged that though I was overjoyed to meet them, they received little consolation in return. They continued to flog themselves in not being able to save both of us. I decided then that the life I continued had to be beyond reproach and of double service to our community. If they couldn't have saved the lives of two, then the one life they did save, would do the work of both.

The rich, ecru iridescent invitation stated the facts:

Michael Joseph Nolte
insists on the pleasure of your company
as he honours the
HEROES & ANGELS
in his life,
six o'clock in the evening
Friday, August 19, 2005
The Ritz Charles
Cocktails, Presentation, Dinner and Dancing.
Black Tie

The party of a lifetime, about a lifetime, for the time of my life was about to happen.

During the weeks of the trial, I would distract myself with the elements of this celebration that would finally allow all these incredible people to come together, meet each other, and most importantly for me to say "Thank you."

What kind of event could I plan if cost were no object?

Cost, of course, became an object. On a more realistic scale, I planned the party celebrating the gift I had received. A second life.

In turn, I now selected gifts for each of the people that I would invite up on stage. Reluctantly I gave up on new cars for Dave and Troy.

Using the song, "Make new friends and keep the old. One is silver and the other gold," I developed a silver and gold theme for table linens, ceiling canopy, place settings, and floral arrangements. Chairs were covered in white linen with silver and gold tiebacks. Each guest received a gold and silver gift bag that contained a blown glass toaster ornament and stand. The story that explained its significance was attached in a little booklet.

I conjured up every good idea I've ever had for clients' events and gratefully accepted every favor and bit of help offered.

Rosebuds were suspended on filament from the chandeliers and elevated arrangements of white lilies and tall grasses soared above the tables. The stage was enhanced with obelisks of votive lights that twinkled as the lights would dim for the various video montages and slide shows I had created.

Out of the 1,000 names on the first guest list, I developed three filters to make the "A List," and I explained them at the opening of the presentation. A. You played a significant role in this journey. B. You won't poke fun at the transparency that would be present. C. We intend to have a lifelong relationship with you after tonight.

The 250 guests followed this unique evening in a silver and gold program. Over the course of three hours, I invited these special people to meet the "Heroes and Angels" in my life as I explained who they were and what they had done.

Coming together were my three post-college roommates who hadn't all been in one room since they were groomsmen in my wedding a quarter of a century ago, Pete Emrick, Randy Frazier, Tom Kempker; my three favorite girl cousins (two of which hadn't seen each other in 30 years) Carol Duncan, JoAnn Stephan, Teri Kay Willett; Barbie's grade-school chums, Paula Callis, Mary Ellen Bechtel, Sherry Shelton, Paula Wiemholt: 25 friends of Dave and 25 friends of Troy.

My talented friend, Steve Courtney, led the audience in singing, "Faith, Hope and Love" and "Servant Song." The string quartet led by Alex Shum played in conjunction with Dorothy Brandwein on the piano. It was part family reunion, revival, rejoicing, and all of it unique. As I said, "How many people live through what I have and are able to say thank you to all the people that mattered so much – all in one room."

The first set of surprised honorees were introduced and presented with flowers. The second set was invited to come on stage and received a little gift. The words of response they offered at the podium echoed in the room with nuances that I never knew or realized. The sharing was going both ways.

Those I thanked on stage included:

Our incredible neighbors, Chuck and Sandi Cantor who took "Love thy neighbor" to a whole new level.

Cathy's sister, Charlene, and her husband Jonathan Finck. They represented the very beginning of the saga and in spite of their own loss, stood beside us.

Our siblings, Jennifer Nolte, Sherry Nolte Starke and Chris Zeller, who cared for our daughters and supported us like only family can. (Barbie's sisters Paula and Donna were not able to attend.)

Steve and Phil, my best guy friends who were so constantly there.

Mom and Dad, nothing more need be said there.

Judy and Connie, the former employees, now like family, first to the E.R.

Lyria Bartlett, the owner of the B&B that housed my family for what became longer than anyone could have imagined.

Our Prayer Group, whose multiple trips to the burn unit brought a 4th of July picnic to my room, almond M&Ms, and applause when I could stand for two minutes.

My legal team, Grant, Scott, Tom, and Doug. Patience and expertise x 4.

My medical team headed by Dr. Terry. (Standing ovation. No surprise.)

The Adrians – they had their own slideshow. (I couldn't risk trying to talk about them without choking up.)

Barbie introduced the wives of my lifesavers and gave them Swarovski crystal hearts.

And finally, the two everyone wanted to meet – Dave and Troy!

It was incredible! The music swelled, the crowd stood, and the tears flowed.

Dave spoke for both of them. My daughters presented them with oil paintings that depicted the Biblical story of The Good Samaritan and I had a brass plate engraved on each gilt frame:

To David Bryan/To Troy Brinkoetter

Thank you for being my Good Samaritan

May 22, 2003... Love, Michael Nolte

Then I asked their daughters to come forward. Machelle Bryan and Kelanie and Brooke Brinkoetter were dressed like princesses. I explained to the girls how brave their fathers had been that day. I told them that they had done for me something no one else would or could. I told them that the one thing I could do to thank them was to do for them what no one else could.

And out came the bridal veils and the wedding march started playing!

Depending on their wish list and my ability at the time, those weddings are mine to make happen, and it will be a pleasure.

But before there's a wedding, I know there is college. I told their fathers that hopefully that expense is going to be a little lighter as I had asked the guests to substitute a "bottle of wine" type hostess gift for this evening and instead contribute to the scholarship foundation I had established for each of the girls and for Tyler Newton. I thought Dave and Troy were going to buckle at the knees.

Just as the presentation was wrapping up and people had stood to leave, I acted as if I had forgotten someone and asked everyone to remain seated for a second.

The true combination of both "Hero and Angel" was the lady in the front row wearing the purple satin ball gown. The room went dim as Josh Groban started singing "You Raise Me Up" and a montage of our 25 years of loving each other started to play. At its conclusion, Barbie joined me on stage for one of the most beautiful, impromptu speeches she's ever given in her life.

I had told people for months that the person who truly deserved a Purple Heart through all this wasn't me, but rather Barbie, and I surprised her that evening with one.

I had found an 80-carat (representing the year of our wedding, 1980) heart-shaped amethyst and had it surrounded by 25 diamonds (representing the number of years we were married). Its bail was a tiny heart of 12 smaller diamonds that symbolized the continued months that I hope we always have to add to the years below and all of it was suspended on triple herringbone chains, symbolizing our three daughters. The chains were of silver and gold, representing our friends, both new and old.

That was the fitting conclusion to the presentation and we led the group to the ballroom where dinner was served. Dancing was enjoyed with my all time favorite band, Atlantic Express, playing. The evening was a long time coming, everything I had ever hoped and too short in its glory.

The next morning lots of the out-of-towners came to the house for brunch. Dr. and Mrs. Terry came as well, which gave even more people a chance to thank him for what he had done for our family. Curtis and Rochelle Marsh capably worked as social coordinators for all the festivities and they slipped out that afternoon with the kitchen cleaner than when we started, just as I crashed into bed at 3 p.m.

What a weekend!

I had joy, joy, joy, joy down in my heart,

down in my heart,

down in my heart.

TWELVE
Seek First to Understand (or the Book of Daniel)

As the months rolled along that first year, I found myself always recalling how many months since the injury. Then at the six-month mark, I started thinking of how many months until the first anniversary. What had I been doing this week last year? How about this day a year ago?

As the dreaded first anniversary came due, I thought maybe I should distract myself until it was over. My psychologist counseled me to face it and create a ritual that would provide some release that this day, May 22, had on me. Those plans developed right along with what the State of Missouri Highway Patrol had in mind as well.

They opted to create a memorial week for Officer Newton and highlight the importance of the state law, "Pass with Care." Many volunteered their time to double up as they stung lots of travelers with tickets over the holiday weekend. The memorial week opened with a service and press conference in the Higginsville, Missouri, city hall, two miles from the crash site. I was invited to attend.

Knowing that I wanted to place a wreath at the crash site, I shopped for days to find the one nice enough, big enough, quality enough to do this anniversary justice. None were available, so I made one myself. The local news stations called wondering if I remembered that it was the first anniversary of the wreck. ??????

Both Shonnie and I wanted to be at the crash site at 6:50 a.m. I deferred of course to her wishes and agreed, via lawyers, to stop by on my way to the city hall service at 9 a.m. The civil trial had not started yet, thus the same "no speak" rule was in place if we were near each other in the room.

When I arrived at the site it was apparent that a lot of people had remembered what day it was. Dozens of blue and white balloons were tethered to the freshly painted cross. The grass had been manicured with a push mower and bouquets of fresh flowers were lying at the foot of the cross. I placed my wreath of red and white roses and a blue bow on an easel. On the card I simply wrote, "May what happened here a year ago make a difference. Michael Nolte"

The first time I stopped and touched the cross – nine months after the crash – I threw up. As time went by, I was relieved that the sweating anxiety attacks that used to accompany the crash site had abated. Now I simply stood there feeling the blasts of wind as trucks blew by. I couldn't believe I had survived that impact.

At City Hall, I learned that the emotions of the morning had proved Shonnie's undoing and she had retreated back to her new home in Newburg, Missouri. (She had re-located to the farm owned by the Newtons and built the house she and Mike had planned.) So there was no chance of conversation.

As a result though, I became the only representative of the crash and I think it meant a lot to the troopers that I stayed for the service. The governor was there as well, issuing the proclamation of the Memorial Week. He sat beside me as "Amazing Grace" was sung. Gut wrenching.

I had brought fresh white roses to offer to Shonnie. In her absence, I stopped a second time by the cross as I headed home. I thought I might as well leave them for Mike. As I lingered this time, I looked closely at some of the memorial offerings left by his friends. There were still several laminated photos that had hung from the little tree that his parents had brought at Christmas, now thumb tacked to the cross. I saw him smiling, laughing, with Tyler, with his sister Kris, with his parents. At his funeral, photo buttons had been made and were worn by friends. (We had done those for Micah as well.) Many of these buttons were at the crash site this day. One was suspended by Mardi Gras beads up high by the replica of his badge. I looked into his face and found myself finally talking to him.

"Mike, I can stand here and pray, bawl or throw up for the rest of my life, and it's not going to bring you back. If I'm going to make any good come out of this though, I'm going to have to let that moment 'go.' For the sake of my own family I have to move forward."

As I safely returned to my garage, alone (like I had planned to do a year ago this day), I breathed a huge sigh of relief and the gears in my heart shifted out of "neutral" and into "forward."

Barbie and I went out for a quiet dinner and spent the night at The Fairmont. We just wanted each other. We watched the news reports of the memorial service and saw the clips from a year ago. We just held each other in our arms and gratitude in our hearts. No tears. We were so wiped out by the emotions of the memory and the day's agenda. We slept the deepest we had in a year.

The next morning we ordered breakfast and lovemaking in bed.

We hurried home to our girls.

A page had been turned.

I would always encourage others to not run from anniversaries. I think there is a lot of healing that comes from bracing yourself and then embracing the moment. You have better control of the outcome if you wrap your arms (head) around it. Once that "first" was done, I was a different person. Not "whole"...but a whole lot closer than before May 22, 2004.

I feel like I had met Mike Newton, the trooper. I was invited to a press conference with U.S. Senator Jim Talent as we spoke about the importance of the amendment that he had championed through Congress making "Pass with Care" not just a spotty, state-by-state law, but a national law. On August 11, 2005, President Bush signed the amendment as a part of national highway improvement legislation.

Then just a layman, now a state representative, Jeff Grisamore was the driving force to bring Senator Talent's attention to the wreck. He had known Mike Newton and lived in the area. He was friends with several troopers and felt the ignorance of the law might have made a difference to Paul Daniel's decision to ignore flashing lights on the shoulder. Grisamore didn't want another family going through what the Newtons and Noltes had suffered. I was "the face" of the importance of "Pass With Care." It's a role from which I will not shrink.

Two anniversaries, two Christmases, two birthdays, had come and gone.

The trial was now over. I could live my life without dread of surveillance. The "Heroes and Angels Gala" was a warm memory. I was back at work, still loving my career and approaching each day at warp speed. I was still testing my boundaries. I was very much proving to others – or myself – that I could get back in the saddle and ride. At times I think I was more at a rodeo than a racetrack though. Everything I took on, I over-did.

In the months after the verdict, I looked to finally hear from Paul Daniel. Why? Because if I were in his shoes, that's what I would have done. He had initiated horrific hurt, never apologized, surely saw the outcome on television, and now knew it was safe to approach us.

If there's one major character flaw that I can see clearly in myself, it's the value judgments I place on others. I typically think that others will hold the same values concerning ethics, integrity, honesty, sensitivity, and kindness to others. Or more importantly, they would express their values the same way.

Apparently Paul Daniel wasn't anything like Michael Nolte. That wasn't an easy conclusion to accept.

I remembered his initial rejection of my request for just one hour of his time. I remembered his request for early release (based on good behavior) and sitting behind him again in a courtroom in April 2004, when it was denied. I remembered the call from the jail letting me know he was being released a month later. I assumed he was just skipping back into this life as if it had never happened.

I knew that for me to let go of him, I needed to do the same thing as I had with the crash site cross – I needed to eyeball it and stare it down. I still had my questions and only he had the answers. My friends thought I was nuts trying to find him, but I persisted.

Paul Daniel (even his two first names annoyed me) had moved from New Hampton, Missouri. He had his phones disconnected. Lost his job. Let his vehicle registrations all lapse and didn't own a home. This seemed to be a man who wanted to disappear. It took awhile but I finally got a cell phone number for his father-in-law who told me he would have his daughter call me, and she did.

As soon as I heard her voice on the phone I could see in my mind the news footage of the day of Paul's sentencing. As we passed through the halls of troopers standing at attention, Barbie and I said nothing. Shonnie and the Newtons followed; they said nothing. As we watched this play out on television that evening, next came Paul Daniel and his wife. She was screaming at the press, "Get away. Get away. This is a highly personal time for us." She was putting her hand over the lens. "How Jerry Springer," I remember thinking.

I was revolted by this reaction and remembered yelling at the television, "You think this is a highly personal moment for *you?!* Take a look lady at Mrs. Newton. Take a look at Mrs. Nolte. You want to talk about a 'highly personal moment?' What happened to *their* husbands is a highly personal moment!'"

For two years I harbored a little grudge toward her. Now she was on the phone telling me that my intention of meeting Paul in early December would "just make my Christmas wish list complete. Paul needs this so much!" I just held the phone in my hand and looked at it!

Once again, she pictured her family as the victims!

She further stupefied me with the news that the two of them had been delivering pulpit talks to churches throughout northern Missouri about the wreck. She said, "You ought to come hear us talk sometime. It's really a powerful story!" Again I just looked at the phone! Hear the story? Lady, I lived the story.

When I deduced that they were profiting because of the wreck, my indignation reached new heights. They faxed me a map to their latest home and we agreed on the date of December 11, 2005. What neither of us realized at that time, it would be exactly two years since I had first laid eyes on him.

My trip to see the Daniels though, was the second half of an emotional day. In the morning, I had been invited by Liberty United Methodist Church, to offer a guest speaking spot in recognition of the 50th birthday of one of their beloved choir members – Dave Bryan.

Two days prior, both Dave and Troy had been our guests for my 51st birthday dinner party December 9. They were the only guests I really wanted to celebrate the fact that indeed I was turning another year older. Yahoo! Susan Bryan brought me a loaf of her coveted fresh-baked bread.

Troy sat up a little recorder on the table to help him remember some of the details for Julia, as at the last minute she had to miss the dinner.

(I recalled the many times that in conversations with Troy, he would interrupt and say, "Wait a minute, I've got to turn on my brain." This was all a result of the short-term memory loss he suffered as a result of exposure to Gulf War poison gasses. At 36 years old.)

Pastor Turnbough opened the service with the analogy of how Joseph had served as a hero to Mary in the Christmas story. Her unplanned pregnancy could have been a source of embarrassment for her family and yet Joseph was there for her. Rev. Turnbough transitioned into how each of us could be a hero to others as well if we just were open to the occasion.

I had been seated in the back row behind the tallest man in the congregation. Dave and Susan were in the choir, facing the nave. I kept weaving back and forth behind my "shield" and kept my face down into the hymnal until I heard the minister intro me with the words, "There's a hero among us today and someone here to talk about how he came to step up to the plate when God called."

As I walked down the center aisle, the Bryans were being escorted into the front pew. I couldn't even look at Dave's face as I knew I would never get through the tribute I had prepared if I did. I opened by singing "Happy Birthday to Me." I explained that my family was able to sing that song two days earlier, thanks to the courage of one of the members of their congregation, a window of missing glass and a bonus of 15 seconds. Susan just laid her head on Dave's shoulder and wiped her eyes. Parts of it were hard for the Bryans to hear, but I could tell by the listeners' attention, they had no idea of the magnitude of what he had done.

I drew a parallel between what happened to Dave being akin to the protection God placed around the prophets Shadrach, Meschach, and Abednego when they were thrown into the fiery furnace. King Nebuchadnezzar called them out and "they saw that fire had not harmed their bodies, nor was a hair of their heads singed; their robes were not scorched, and there was no smell of fire on them." Daniel 4:27

In spite of Dave's very physical involvement in the circumstances, he had had such protection. He too was being used by God, specifically to save Michael Nolte that day. Why Dave? Why me?

I shared with the listeners – who were staring at this humble man that had this secret all these months – that at the conclusion of the service I was headed to meet Paul Daniel for the first time. Book of Daniel? Paul Daniel? Coincidence? Exactly two years later?

I asked the congregation to sing "Happy Birthday" to Dave, which they did with gusto. The pastor called the Bryans forward. When Dave approached me with arms outstretched and tried to say "Thank you," I lost my composure and we embraced all through the song. The pastor then laid hands on Dave and me and offered the kindest blessing I think I've ever heard. The choir broke into a closing hymn and we walked out with the pastor. All we needed was a balloon drop and confetti cannons and you would have thought someone had just been elected president.

In the receiving line afterwards, it was so cool to be the foil that deflected the spotlight back onto Dave. His friends approached him with eyes of wonder. I handed each person a roll of LifeSavers: to savor the sweetness of the day and to remember the role that Dave played in my life. It was a "10" on all levels. It was a wonderful birthday beginning and I was honored to do it. Dave shares the same birthday as my daughter Justine, December 14. Coincidence?

The lightness of the morning took a turn for the somber as I headed north out into nowhere. My drive to the home of Paul Daniel gave me an additional couple of hours to finally compose my thoughts as to exactly what I wanted from this trip.

I approached this visit with equal parts trepidation and anticipation.

I recalled a photograph of Pope John Paul II visiting his assassin in jail and granting his pardon. As Barbie fretted about my instance to go this alone, I assured her that the visit wasn't going to be long. There would be none of that "papal visit to the jail" scenario.

Leaving highway for county road, blacktop for gravel. Gravel for dirt. I ended up in the middle of nowhere at the base of a windswept slope, topped by the home of the monster who had caused us so much pain.

As I stopped to catch my breath, I realized there wasn't a single other house in sight. I checked my cell phone. No service. If indeed this redneck blew me away with a sawed-off shotgun, no one would ever know where I was. They would never find my body. (The labels were flying through my head.)

The house was a rental property that was part modular/part mobile. There was no obvious front door and no sidewalk. I knew when I climbed out of my SUV, I would re-enter it a changed man.

Paul opened the door under a fiberglass patio cover and shook my left hand. I instantly thought "How weird. He doesn't even know how to shake hands properly."

Kathy came in to introduce their daughters who were five and eight. The Daniels are both big people. Paul's jeans and socks even looked brand new. I respected their obvious efforts to clean up like we all would for company. (There I sat in my Ralph Lauren black suit, fresh from church, looking like someone from the FBI.)

The children disappeared and Kathy appropriately left as I had asked earlier. The house, though not furnished or decorated well, was immaculately clean. They had a small tree up and only two Christmas cards taped to the wall. As I took off my watch to lay it on the coffee table, I told Paul of my intention to be out of his life in 60 minutes.

Then the dynamic changed.

He replied, "Mr. Nolte, after what I did to you, my time is yours. You stay as long as you want. If you want to talk all afternoon, we can. You're welcome to stay for supper and we can talk some more. If you would like to sleep over, we could continue in the morning." Maybe there was something deeper here than I had surmised.

I told him of my intention of "Seeking first to understand and then be understood." I explained my theory of the ripple effect and of choices and consequences. He seemed to get all three concepts. I asked permission to lead the conversation with asking him questions by which I may better come to understand him and what happened then and since then. He agreed. He said, "I'll answer anything you ask me."

Since I expected to have about 30 minutes to ask him questions and since I am the ultimate list maker, I came prepared – having written exactly 15 questions on a manila folder.

The questions I had prepared tumbled out.

1. In 10 minutes tell me your bio: family of origin, schooling, hobbies, marriages, parental relationships, jobs, goals.

2. What in the hell were you thinking that day? His answer? Probably the only one I could believe, "I wasn't."
3. Describe what happened. I've heard from crash experts and eyewitnesses. I need to hear from your perspective. (This caused him to choke up a bit, but I pushed on.)
4. What was the ripple effect in your life when you came home that day?
5. How did you feel the day of your sentencing?
6. Describe jail.
7. Why did you petition for early release when your sentence was only six months?
8. How was your homecoming?
9. How has your choice of driving behavior affected your marriage, your fathering, your job, your church life, your extended family?
10. Did you track the case – the wreck, my homecoming, the trial, the verdict, the reunion with Dave and Troy – in the media?
11. How did you feel about the verdict we received?
12. What bothered you most these last two years?
13. How did you feel about my coming today?
14. Why did you walk and not run from your truck? Why didn't you try to get us out?
15. Why did you never reach out to us? Why no contact with Shonnie or Barbie?

Paul attended 19 schools in 12 years as an Army brat. He made his best grades in ROTC. No college. No money – ever. His mother gave birth to an African American baby while still married to Paul's white father. The father split when Paul was a senior. The mother took Paul and his half-sister to live with her mother in New Hampton. Paul eventually returned to Arkansas to live with friends until he graduated. He married at 20 a 28-year-old drug addict. He had many affairs – one that resulted in his first daughter with Kathy. He couldn't marry her though, as he was still married to wife No. 1, but she wouldn't grant him a divorce until he paid off all her illegal drug bills. He and Kathy eloped four months after the baby was born. She comes from a strict Baptist family and they hated Paul. They've been married eight years. He had been a drunk. He has never held a job more than nine months. He is estranged from his mother, but close to one of two brothers who lives nearby. He and Kathy met at Wal-mart where they both worked and are from the same rural areas.

He answered every question in depth and I do believe, honestly. What I learned by his responses was truly a walk in his shoes. I received illumination and softening. I guess it's called understanding.

By illumination, I mean light being cast into areas I didn't know about. It was the fleshing out of details that no one had told me completely. By softening, I mean, I saw his humanness, not just an awfulness.

Does that make me want to say, "Gosh, in light of that, maybe I've exaggerated this a bit? Maybe it wasn't so bad. See ya."

No way!

I was most interested to learn why he never contacted Shonnie or Barbie.

His lawyer had advised him to not contact either family and, to underscore that, he told him the Newtons had issued a public statement saying they would never forgive Paul "and probably the Noltes feel the same way." (Both were untruths.)

He was astonished to learn that a note would have meant so much to us. I pointed out seven different times over the course of two years, when it would have been much appreciated.

"I wish I ignored my lawyer's advice."

His parole ended December 15, (in four days), two years from when he started to serve time. He was afraid, not knowing me, that if he wrote, I might turn the letter over to my lawyers and it would be viewed as breaking parole and cause to throw him back in jail. He's a very simple thinker yet had a deep vocabulary and was an excellent communicator.

At one point Kathy came back in and started holding and patting his hand. It bugged me. This was supposed to be just man to man.

But I thought I'd let it go if she just listened and didn't talk.

She talked.

I asked her to leave.

She did.

When it was my turn, I told him how disappointed and frustrated I was that he had rejected my request for an earlier meeting. I told him how turned off I was by his hand wringing and hangdog look and Kathy's "we're the victims here" behavior. He said he wished he could completely re-do that horrible day and felt like a rabbit being led out to a pack of wolves. He would have felt better if he could have been handcuffed in a chair and I would have just come up and beat the shit out of him. I really believe he meant that.

I told him that I didn't refer to May 22 as "an accident" and was offended that he did. I gave the example: A child in a tire swing gets killed when a limb breaks off the tree and hits him in the head. That's an accident.

Driving a truck in the manner he did is a choice. The wreck was completely avoidable.

It was a wreck.

He agreed on all counts and apologized. When he later slipped and said "accident," he caught himself and apologized again.

I asked if he wanted to hear of the ripple effect of his choice in my life. He did. I told him briefly of the experiences I had being air-lifted, the horror of that first day for my family and friends, the debridement, the skin harvesting, the surgeries, the inability to bear weight, the learning to walk, operate a wheelchair and walker, and go through months of rehab. I didn't focus on the pain or the hallucinations. Just the objective parts.

I asked him if he wanted to see some photos. He replied, "I think I should." I allowed Kathy back in. And then they did something that really nobody else has ever done and I learned from them a valuable lesson.

As I handed them the edited stack of 8x10s, they held each one carefully by the edges or on their palms (so as not to smudge) and studied each image a long time. Upon viewing the crushed car and my unrecognizable face, they held them between them, touched their heads together and tears started dripping off their full cheeks.

I excused myself to the bathroom to give them a little private time. Here was the evidence of the destruction he had started.

Oftentimes when people have asked to see pictures, I get a sense of "Okay, done that. Too much information." or "Look at how good you're doing now."

They act like the past never happened.

When I returned from the bathroom, when they could have just put them all in the "been seen" pile, they hadn't. They were just finishing up. They showed respect for the damage to my body. They didn't try to brush it off or diminish it in any way. As Doug Mitchell commented later, "They showed reverence." And they did.

I examine my own past with how many times someone had shown me pictures that were very important to them and I kept talking about other things the entire time I held them in my hands. How many times was I irreverent? And if there have ever been pictures that someone wouldn't want to see, it would be those, by that couple. I was touched.

Nobody talked much after that. I asked him if there was anything he wanted to ask me. He replied, "Can you think of anything I can do to make you feel better about what I've done?"

Complete ownership. I was stunned.

I told him there were two things, the first being to write letters to the Newtons and my family. He said he already had them started and he was planning to mail them December 15.

He told me he can't go to the crash site. He can't drive the interstate. Too many flashbacks. I told him I used to have the same anxieties. I had some suggestions to overcome those very real fears.

I asked him about their future plans. Kathy is a special education teaching assistant 20 minutes away. Paul has stayed on his present job of installing trailers now for two years. He hates it, but the money is good.

I couldn't leave without asking about their perceived exploitations of the wreck by getting hired as motivational speakers. I learned that several churches stepped up to pay their utility bills and donated groceries while he was incarcerated. Someone even paid Kathy's tuition to finish her B.A. Upon release, they felt it was important to go to these churches and express their thanks. I know that feeling.

The "thank you" then evolved into a complete witness talk about the screw-ups in their lives and the bad choices they have made. The wreck for them was the defining moment in which they could only rely on each other and turned to God for help. They now caution people, particularly the youth, to drive more carefully before they create a tragedy. The payment they receive is a free will offering taken after the talk. I didn't even tell Kathy how far from that she had sounded. I told them I would like to be in their next audience.

The visit was over. When I checked my watch, I had been there for four hours. I had listened for three and shared for one. I was completely fine with that ratio.

The mission had been accomplished – or so I thought. I had walked in his shoes.

As I gathered my things and walked to the door, Paul hauled himself off the couch and followed me. He kept his head down as he spoke, "You said there were two things I could do for you. You only gave me one, the letter writing. What is the second?"

That conversation had been 20 minutes ago! Truthfully, there wasn't a second thing.

To stall for time, I asked him why he had shaken my left hand when I first arrived.

Weird question...but it just popped out of my mouth.

His reply changed my life. "I think you would only shake hands the right way with someone you regard as a friend or want to have as a friend. I knew you wouldn't think of me that way. Plus, I didn't feel worthy to shake your right hand."

The rubber had just met the road. The sheep were being separated from the goats. The men were being separated boys, the wheat from the chaff, and every other cliché that had ever been uttered at such moments.

His words were like the finger of God on my chest. The moment he said "...not worthy to shake your hand...," I instantly thought of the story of the apostle who felt unworthy to loosen the sandal of Jesus. And ringing in my head were the words of the prayer I had been reciting as I lay burning in the pasture next to the Crown Vic.

"...forgive us as we forgive those who have trespassed against us...."

Paul didn't feel worthy to shake my right hand!? Why did he have to word it that way?

I thought, "Okay, 'Mr. Christian.' Do you walk the walk or just talk the talk?"

Decision made. No turmoil. Just a calm that came over me, and words I had never formed in my head started coming out of my mouth.

I told him to stop looking at the floor and look me in the eye.

I told him the second thing was to listen to my parting words, but first I wanted him to give me his hand...his right hand.

His big, calloused paw swallowed mine. He still looked at the floor. "Look up. Look me square in the eyes," I said.

He did. And when he did, his eyes started to water.

Then I said, "Here are the words I want you to hear come from me."

I gulped and the next 10 words came out of my mouth slowly, deliberately and carefully chosen.

"Paul," I said. "I forgive you, for what you did to me."

All 300-plus pounds of him came down on my shoulder. He broke into sobs and kept saying over and over and over, "Thank you. Thank you. Thank you." He hugged me so tightly I literally couldn't inhale. I leaned against the doorjamb to support our combined weight. Kathy was leaning over the back of the couch sobbing too.

"You're a good man, Paul," I continued. "You just made a bad choice."

"The wreck is behind both of us. It will never happen again. I want you to go on with your life and make some good happen for somebody else."

I never broke down once.

He followed me out to my car – in his brand new socks – and stood in the cold mud, completely unaware of the chill and the wetness beneath his feet. I told him that we probably would never see each other again, but that if he wanted to stay connected, I was fine with that.

As I finished a three-point turn around, I opened the passenger window and spoke to him over the empty seat, "Paul, Merry Christmas to you and your family." He replied, "Merry Christmas to you, Mr. Nolte."

I drove off into the twilight.

It was done.

I was totally fine. It wasn't the drama of the Holy Father forgiving his assassin in prison, but there was a shadow of that emotion. I never went there thinking that would be the conclusion. It all just evolved so naturally, that to say those words was really easier than if I had forced it. There was a lightness in my chest in the sense that I could check off one more folder in the file cabinet of this life experience.

All my life I knew the importance of the words, "I love you."

I raised my girls to remember to say, "Thank you" and "I'm sorry."

I called my parents and told them of what had transpired. Mom said it simply, "We are very proud of you, son." Those are important words too.

Now at the beginning of my second life, I learned the power of the words, "I forgive you."

THIRTEEN
The Two Mikes

Paul Daniel mailed both letters to us and Barbie read hers to the girls. Was it written the way I would have? No. Did that make it wrong? No. Did he say he was sorry? Over and over.

The second letter was to the Newtons and I had promised Paul that I would personally deliver it and witness that they at least read it once. I started to orchestrate that visit right after Christmas. Finally in April 2006, it was on the calendar.

I don't know if Bobbie Newton dreaded or welcomed the thought of me coming to see her. Maybe both and her actions indicated that.

Mike's dad, Gary, was the groundskeeper for the highway patrol. His father had been a cook at the training academy. For the Newtons, having a son become an officer was a pinnacle. Losing him in the line of duty was the demolition of a dream.

Gary retreated inside himself and refused to attend any of the memorial services, in Higginsville, in Washington D.C., at Troop A headquarters in Lee's Summit, in Jefferson City and was rarely in the courtroom during the trial.

When investigator Doug Mitchell, and Shonnie's lawyer, J. Kent Emison, came to prepare them for trial, Gary would leave the house. I was told he had started drinking again, and I knew that was to dull the pain. I suspect that Bobbie's on-again, off-again decision to receive me was due to pressure from him.

Though they were slightly younger than I, the experience had aged them considerably. The day I made the four-hour trip, Gary had decided to go hunting and not take his grandsons with him, as originally promised. As Bobbie called that morning and told me of that new development "We're going to be stuck watching my grandsons if that's okay."

Barbie urged me to not back out.

Once again I designed a wreath. This one in blue hydrangeas. What was this? My sixth? Seventh? I had sent photos of each one placed by the cross to the Newtons. I wanted them to know I remembered. That somebody still cared. I never heard from them.

I decided to treat the Newtons the way I would want the Noltes treated by the Newtons if the circumstances had been reversed. If Dave and Troy had gone to the driver's side first. If the glass would have broken. If the 15 seconds could have been spent on the other side of the car. If Shonnie was still the wife and Barbie now the widow.

My parents and Barbie formed a friendship with the Newtons during the five weeks of sharing lunch in the private witness room during the trial. They were very comfortable with each other. But the element that bound them together was missing – their "two Mikes."

As much as I hated to tell the jury the details of what went on inside the car that day, it wasn't because I was afraid to re-live it. I wanted Jim Feeney, Ford's lawyer, to hear every single word about the avoidable horror his company had caused.

I dreaded having the Newtons hear it. Mid-way through, Bobbie and Shonnie burst into tears and ran from the courtroom. It was as bad as I had imagined.

Now 10 months had passed and I made my way through beautiful countryside, stopping occasionally at Catholic churches along the way to light a candle, to say a prayer, to keep me focused. St. Joseph's in Westphalia, Holy Family in Freeburg, Visitation of our Lady in Vienna, all beautiful old churches built by Germans long ago in search of farmland in mid-America.

When I pulled up to the rural setting of the Newtons' modular home, I could see the grandsons playing ball in the front yard. Bobbie welcomed me warmly. She asked about my returning to work and stated that they had had no idea of how badly I had been burned. She had indeed received some consolation in knowing that if her Mike had had to live with the limitations that kept him out of the sun, off the ball field, unable to fish, swim, run, or in constant pain, he was definitely in a better place.

With the casual voice one would invite a guest to survey a quilting project, she asked if I would like to see the room for Mike that she had been working on. For the next two hours I sat on the bed as she showed me this Smithsonian that she had created as a legacy for Tyler. She had filed, categorized, laminated, and framed every certificate, letter of condolence, proclamation, and photograph the family had received.

She showed me a footlocker filled with labeled plastic bags that contained elements from his living and his dying. They covered everything from the newborn outfit in which he was brought home from the hospital to a few business cards found in the glove box of the Crown Victoria.

He had just received several hundred and they were packed tightly in the box. All were destroyed except these few in the center and the edges of each were burned away. It was all that remained of the car's contents. I asked her if I might have one and she gave it to me. His business card is in my Bible with all the other holy cards collected through the years from funerals of loved ones.

One of the plastic bags contained something she was at first reluctant to talk about but held it with such love that I knew it was of great importance to her. She explained that after the first memorial service at the crash site, just days after the wreck and before the funeral, she had waited until the crowds left and felt the need to connect with the exact spot where her baby had died. She crawled in the burned grass just feeling the earth. Primal? Maybe? Have I been in her shoes and felt the comfort that might bring? Not at all.

Suddenly she found a piece of bone and gristle and hid it under her rain poncho. She asked the funeral director to identify it, and he told her it was a right femur bone singed with gunpowder. That all made sense, as Mike's pistol had exploded on his hip and his right leg had been blown off. This was a piece of her child and she treasured it like a relic.

I gave her Paul Daniel's letter and asked her to read it in my presence so I could fulfill my promise to him. She did and then handed it to me. It was much like that to my family. Typed. Two paragraphs. Rather non-specific, but at least more than he had offered before. (I later learned that Gary had indeed destroyed it before reading it.)

She showed me albums of Mike's life. His shoes, his uniform. The inevitable was coming (I could feel it) and it was the moment for which I made the trip.

She acknowledged that he was an "eager beaver," anxious to make a good impression on his superiors by writing a lot of tickets. She didn't apologize for that. It wasn't her place.

And we never discussed the feelings expressed by the public, or my own, about being pulled over for such a frivolous excuse. It was irrelevant.

She admitted that at first she was mad at me for "causing him to pull off on the shoulder" but later accepted that he did it everyday and that the decision to do so for this infraction was his choice, not someone else's. She was relieved to hear of my urging people to wait for a safe pull-off spot.

But as she leaned across the room I could have guessed her next words and been right. "The coroner, the undertaker, the lawyers, all have different theories of what happened inside that car and how long he was alive after the explosion. What I need to know, and you're the only one I'll believe is, did he suffer?"

As I told her exactly what happened (some of which she had missed in the courtroom), I stressed the fact that neither of us moved or made any sound. I believe that the shock of the explosion shut our minds off from registering any feelings – fear, dread, pain. I could look her in the eye and honestly tell her, "No Bobbie. I know he didn't feel a thing. He never suffered."

There was a long pause as that truth floated into her heart. I said nothing more. She wiped her cheeks and hugged me in relief. "A huge weight has just lifted out of me."

We drove two miles to the cemetery where Mike was laid to rest. She re-lived the majesty of the burial with the trumpets, the honor guard, the hundreds of people. She showed me on her waist how high the flowers were piled after his coffin was lowered into the grave.

Seeing the tombstone made it all real to me, finally. There was the date, May 22, 2003, engraved into black granite with a name sounding much like my own. In tribute to his love of fishing, the painted illustration showed a couple in a boat with the man catching "the big one." In her grief, Shonnie had approved the proof before catching the error of the spelling, the "a" and "e" had been transposed. Bobbie told me she wanted to spell Mike's formal name differently "just to make him stand out." I had noticed the back and forth of that spelling in newspapers, television, framed certificates. Now I know which was truly correct – Micheal – but forever in granite it will be spelled like my own – Michael.

There were no tears on my part as I placed the hydrangea wreath at the grave. I simply studied all the illustrations and information. There was even a photo of Mike and Shonnie on their wedding day. It crept into my sub-conscious why my sister Sherry had dragged her feet so long in getting Micah's tombstone ordered.

You only need a tombstone for someone when they are really, really dead. Micah was dead. And now Mike Newton was dead. The hidden hope that maybe, just maybe, all of this had been a ruse, a cover-up, and Mike had been just so badly burned that he was hidden away in a burn unit in the Bahamas just so Shonnie could collect his life insurance money was over.

Micheal Lynn Newton had burned to death. Michael Joseph Nolte had not.

As we returned to the Newtons' home, Shonnie arrived with her new husband. She and Mark were returning from Las Vegas where they were married the day prior while flying over the city in a helicopter. Mike's sister Kris and her husband were their witnesses. I presented her a wedding gift that Barbie had sent along and told her that before I left I needed something from her.

I told her of the increasing number of invitations to share my story and that corporations and groups were willing to compensate me for doing so. They found it not motivational, but rather inspirational. I told her of my feelings of unworthiness in accepting money for a story that was built on her tragedy and I wanted to know if I had her blessings to do so. She looked at me and said, "Absolutely, something good has to come of this. It could help people."

I then told her of the scholarship foundation that was started for Tyler and her eyes were watering, "You don't have to do that." I replied, "It's the only way I can accept the money." In retrospect, I'm glad the interruptions of the boys running in and out caused the quick conversation to happen in that order. I received her blessings before she knew of the scholarship.

I felt very out of place at that point. We posed for a quick photo and there was talk of getting together sometime in the future. The ride home was much lighter and shorter.

I think the trip had been well conceived and well received. My spirit was on the mend.

FOURTEEN
Heart-Shoes

"I know how much you're hurting right now.
If I could, I'd take the pain away. But I can't.
So instead I'm praying that God will provide
you with "heart-shoes" strong enough
to withstand even the sharpest stones."
                    – Charles Spurgeon

What an appropriate metaphor for a guy who can barely walk..."heart-shoes." The pain that the insightful poet has to be referring to, is not that of burned feet and legs, but rather has to be pain of the heart, of the mind, of the soul.

The "heart-shoes" that God did indeed provide for me was when He knew I would be crawling on all fours a long time before I could walk upright again. He gave me four heart-shoes and named them...Barbie, Emma-Lea, Justine, and Caroline.

As much as this story has been about one man's challenges with adversity and how he worked through them, the process in doing so was only made possible because of these four wonderful women who cradled and cared for their husband and father.

My family was impacted along with me at every step of the journey. They too were the subject of stares, questions, the spotlight, and feeling different. They too felt the social isolation as we became housebound and yet almost a tourist attraction. They too felt the economic worries as we pulled away from entertaining and vacations the way we had in the past.   They too felt the frustration of my depression when I would yell at them after school, "Just go to another level of the house and leave me alone." They too felt the fear of the unknown as we were given a tour of the courtroom the night before the trial and saw seat assignments for all of them and the thick document "Newton/Nolte Vs. Ford Motor Company" sitting on the judge's bench.

My family too felt my rages as on the night I was standing in the shower, with my walker, and couldn't remember how to get over the 6-inch lip that edged the pan. To open the door, the warm water had to be turned off. As I stood there dripping, bleeding, chilling, naked and frustrated, I couldn't organize my plan to shift my weight from one leg to the other and at the same time re-position the walker over the lip so I could get out of the shower. They heard me break down in frustration as I yelled, "I wonder if the man who did this to me is having trouble getting out of his shower tonight?!"

For all my girls it was a very difficult journey. I will be always in their debt as I recall what they too suffered on my account.

For Caroline, being 10 and having both parents suddenly living 100 miles from you for almost two months, was hard. Caroline is my brown-eyed beauty who soaks it all in and seldom processes on location. She observed and absorbed. Her thrust into puberty was unexpected and stressful. She missed her dad, but needed her mom. In just recent months, we watched the incredible documentary of "To Iraq and Back," the story of Bob Woodruff. Part way through she started crying and admitted that it was all too similar to what had happened to us.

That evening Caroline and I laid in her bed, like we used to, like we hadn't in too long and talked about her feelings back then. She said she thinks about getting that call all the time and worries constantly each time I'm driving out of town. Perhaps as a result, Caroline is the one that accompanies me on many speaking engagements. I think hearing the story, makes it absorbable. Finally. She's a cautious child and has no tolerance for friends who make fun of the handicapped.

She told me a year later that a classmate was sitting near us on that first Sunday at Mass. The classmate saw the scabs and raw flesh below my shorts and above the bandages. (I had placed a towel over my quads but it was askew.) Sophia made faces and stuck her finger in her mouth. Caroline said she knew right then that Sophia "wasn't a quality person and would never be a friend." Her estimation was shared by many and her prediction a welcome relief.

Caroline is the defender of the defenseless and the most sensitive to providing whatever she can to help out —brownies, ice water, lotion, pain meds.

Justine was about to start her freshman year of high school. She had taken dance classes since she was three years old. She had auditioned for the dance team at Notre Dame de Sion and didn't make the cut. She was so crushed. This reaction surprised me. It came from the daughter who once told me that it was okay that our neighborhood didn't have trees yet; it made for better kite flying. Justine always looks for the positive.

It was a full year of sitting on the bleachers watching that she realized that if indeed she had made the team that summer, she would have had to drop out. Our family structure was in a shambles from May through August, when she had multi-day practices and dance camp out of town. She wasn't driving yet and we didn't have an extra car to have Emma-Lea take her anyway. God's plan for Justine was to sit out that first year. (She has since made the team all remaining years.)

Justine is her father's daughter. She speaks the truth, frequently. Her spoken words are often influenced by her emotional feelings. I recall too clearly one of those "in-and-out" of consciousness afternoons when Justine was in my ICU room, alone for some reason. She was wearing the appropriate gown, gloves and mask and standing beside my bed, afraid to touch me anywhere. She must have thought I was unconscious but I was just sleeping when I heard her softly crying and saying the words, "Dad, please don't die. I can't imagine my life without you in it." I struggled to lift my eyelids, to see tears staining the front of the mask. Two straight lines of darker blue absorbent paper, just below her beautiful blue eyes.

I had to survive this.

Emma-Lea had just completed her sophomore year. Due to multiple health problems and her own frequent hospitalizations, Emma-Lea has had to grow up much quicker than her peers. As a result she is often more comfortable in the company of adults as opposed to vapid teenagers. In her own terms she is "a tough old bird," and can be depended on to be truthful, helpful and consistent. She internalizes her stress though, and as a result had the kidney imbalance attack in the waiting room as I was being rolled out of recovery the first time.

Emma-Lea is extremely close to her grandparents. She and PoPo Nolte would walk the steps of the hospital everyday for exercise (Dad was recovering from knee replacement surgeries). Emma-Lea stayed with Barbie most of the time and helped her remember the details of who had called, what gifts were delivered, what bills needed to be paid, what problems were brewing at the store and in general served as a well qualified first-born representative of the family.

It wasn't until Notre Dame de Sion asked the three of us to offer the homily for their annual Father-Daughter Mass that I heard from the two oldest some of their feelings and fears in those first days.

All three of my girls participated in the trial and the Heroes and Angels party. They met with reporters many times for articles for local papers, they were present when I spoke for Senator Talent's campaign, when I helped present "Heroic Lifesaving Certificates," and when I received "The Hope and Spirit Award" from the University of Missouri Hospital. They have watched our family knit itself back together and I think will always be stronger and more empathetic because of this experience.

Barbie was the one that kept my heart strong enough to endure the burn treatment. In very close concert with Dr. Terry, she directed my care. She spent day after day by my bedside, often falling asleep sitting up, she was so exhausted from just "being on." As calm as the drugs tried to keep me, I always was very anxious to see my wife each morning. After breakfast, sponge bath, new sheets and gown, I would watch the clock and count the minutes until visiting hours opened and I could hear her flats clicking on the tile floor. Before I would recognize her "Good morning" to the nurse's station, I would recognize her gait.

I literally don't think I would have kept fighting if not for Barbie. The will to live isn't there for a burn victim in that much pain. The desire to return to fullness of life isn't there when the scarring and pain seem so limiting. My body would have healed eventually, but I would have never been able to see the big-picture advantages without her perspective. For the rest of my life, I'll be grateful.

As I turned corners in my healing – physically, mentally, emotionally – there were people placed in my path that required me to use the new tools in my toolbox. One such person was Andy Marso, a 22-year-old senior journalism major at the University of Kansas, who was stricken with bacterial meningitis a month before graduation. His story, carried in the local news, explained that meningitis patients are treated like burn victims. They suffer the deprivation of oxygen to their extremities and the dead flesh is cut away and new skin grafted in its place. Most of the time there's certain amputations.

When I became aware of Andy's situation – his family was from Minnesota, they were displaced with a long hospitalization, his treatment was much like my own – I considered visiting. But I let that be someone else's problem. I didn't know the family.

Then I read of Matt Bellomo, a 31-year-old accountant, who had survived the same disease and had both feet amputated. He did go see Andy and said, "I've been there." I realized that if whoever this Matt guy was could do that, I could haul my lazy, grafted body down to the hospital to give Andy a bit of encouragement.

As Matt told me later, he didn't have the torture of debridement. They just amputated his feet without trying to save them. He felt my insight would be a real help to Andy, and the Marsos said it was. When I first befriended Andy, his pain levels were off the chart. I was so impacted by entering a burn unit and seeing the blackened limbs I nearly fainted. Andy asked me if I dreaded the tank as much as he did? He told me of being in so much pain while he was in there that he couldn't even talk. I remembered all too vividly. I affirmed what he was saying and suggested some ways that helped get through that pain. Afterwards I told his family my story, showed them pictures, showed them my newly grafted skin. Gave them a little hope.

Though Andy did have to have multiple amputations, he is now also hell bent on living life to the fullest he can. He was the commencement speaker the following year and in his address he mentioned the kindness of strangers and how that helped him over the worst days. He singled out Matt and me. Of all the people so involved in his care and all the friends he had made over the course of his life, I was surprised to learn what a difference just one more person can make.

Since then, I've visited the patients in the burn unit every time I've been in the hospital. Every time it makes me sick at my stomach. Every time I remember. Just like seeing a trooper pulling a car off on the side of the road, I remember. Just like seeing a crash and burn sequence in a movie, I remember. Just like hearing of a family suffering an unexpected tragic loss of a loved one, I remember.

I help out now with both the local "Gift of Life" program and "Transplant Speakers International." Both raise the awareness of the need for organ donation. Every 30 seconds someone dies in the United States waiting for an organ. Skin is our largest organ and because of myths and misconceptions, is the one least often donated. I have the unique perspective of experience on both sides of the operating room. I am considered both a donor uncle and a tissue recipient.

How full circle is that realization that the one organ that I discouraged my sister, Sherry, to donate was the single organ that I needed? If someone hadn't made the decision to donate the skin, bone and tissue of their loved one, I wouldn't have my legs. As I related this coincidence at a speaking engagement in Durham, North Carolina, for the first time, it seemed like suddenly it all made sense. Without a doubt, I knew the purpose of my life for that day.

As I launch/lurch into my new life, I ask "for what purpose?" each day. I am keenly aware that our time here on earth is pre-determined by God. He has a plan for how we are to use those days and hopefully we'll be open to seeing those possibilities. When our mission on earth is up, when we've touched all the lives we're supposed to touch and lifted up as many people that intersect with our own orbits, He takes us back where we started. I think maybe we're like a good book from God's library. He loans it to Earth for awhile, maybe 80 plus years. When everyone that is supposed to read it has done so, He retrieves it for His own reading pleasure.

In the early months friends would marvel at the mysteries, the miracles associated with my rescue and recovery. They encouraged me to write a book. What would I write about? Why would anybody want to read it? I ignored the possibility for three years.

Now that the narcotic fog has lifted and I can think more clearly, I see the reaction of listeners. I read the notes they send me after hearing the story or reading a newspaper article. They tell me it lifts them up. That's what it's all about. That's why I've written this narrative now.

If I were to stuff the pain of this experience in a box and refuse to examine it again, no one benefits and God wasted a tragedy on a guy that didn't gain from it.

Could I do for spinal cord injured patients what Christopher Reeve did? Never.

Could I do for sufferers of Parkinson's Disease what Michael J. Fox is doing? In my dreams.

But what I – Michael J. Nolte – can do is share my story. Not just with burn victims themselves, but also with critical care nurses, physical therapists, occupational therapists, insurance providers, long-term care providers, and those considering organ donation. I believe all these people, in particular, and the people they love, in general, can benefit from reading about my experiences as a burn victim.

And what about the people just starting their own lap in the race to regain what I call "fullness of life?"

I will tell them about the regular guy who had the Norman Rockwell life. I'll mention that somewhere along the way in his seemingly perfect life, he was horribly burned.

And most importantly, I'll talk about how he got better.

His was the story of a man that was burned...but not broken.

AFTERWORD

I would never wish for any wife to be awakened by the Highway Patrol telling you your husband is being air lifted to the burn unit, get there quickly. That call changed the course of our marriage. And yet, while time stopped for the Nolte family, life continued on around us, oblivious to our trauma. It was an abrupt adjustment. I can't imagine how much harder it would have been if my Mike too would have died.

But we realize our family was also blessed. We were inundated with support of family, friends, and even acquaintances we barely knew. The outpouring of caring in the form of flowers, gifts, monetary donations, cards, visits, meals, and shelter will be something I will never forget. I can only hope to emulate that example when given the chance to be the "giver" and not the recipient. In spite of the distance, our friends in Kansas City remained constantly our lifeline. Our second blessing was that we had in Columbia (where we spent our early married years), a tremendous support group of old friends and co-workers that reached out like there had never been a gap.

With a disaster such as ours, there are no experiences upon which to draw. There's no proto-type of "This is what you do when your husband is in the Burn Unit for more than two months." As a nurse, I had a slight advantage in that I could navigate, with a little confidence, the hospitalization experience. I was included in the truth each day by an incredible doctor and top-drawer nurses. However, nothing can prepare you for the reactions of your children when they see the dad they love, swollen beyond recognition and bandaged from head to toe. It was frightening for all of us...and, unfortunately, happening to US.

My advice to spouses of the critically injured? Trust your doctors, appreciate your nurses, and yet be sure you are heard. I always believed that Mike would get better. He has been a fighter ever since I fell in love with him. He fights to make better the relationships he values. He fights for the underdog who needs a champion. He fights to initiate improvements all the time: home, professional circles, friendships, church, our family... I knew he would fight with his body to get better. He is never satisfied with the status quo. (That still drives me a little crazy, but what a life I've enjoyed because of his drive.)

I lived each of those days in the Burn Unit with no expectation of the next. I tried to support my in-laws that I love tremendously and my daughters who were scared. I fully supported Dr. Terry's recommendations to heal Mike. At each day's end, I was exhausted and yet couldn't sleep. I gained too much weight in stress eating. Each evening I just had to turn the whole mess over to God. I couldn't have made it those 10 weeks and years beyond without Him.

Fast forward to the present now. Mike is working as much as he can – still coping with significant pain in his legs, ankles and feet every single day. He hasn't fully accepted his disability or the pain levels as he has reasoned that when he finishes the present bottle of morphine, he'll be finished with the pain. He's let the prescription run out with dire consequences five times now. He refuses to get the permanent handicap license plate that marks his car as driven by a disabled man. Instead he has to keep re-applying for the temporary mirror hangtags. He never parks in a handicap zone, leaving it for someone in worse condition, unless he really needs it.

He really misses the sun, the beach and the pool. After 27 years, he still relishes his career of helping engaged couples and their parents feel like guests at their own weddings. But his experiences as a burn victim have re-shaped his focus. He is driven with an intense desire to give back to those in similar situations. Writing this book is a part of that effort and it is, unfortunately, a true story.

He has visited the burn units at both the University of Missouri and University of Kansas hospitals when he thought he could help. As a donor tissue recipient, he has spoken both locally and nationally on behalf of organ donation awareness. As a beneficiary of disability insurance, he has spoken to insurance professionals from around the globe on the benefits of insuring your paycheck. He has created a wallet card urging people to wait for a safe place to pull over to protect the life of the cop and the driver. They are being requested weekly and appreciated by all law enforcement.

People easily relate to him on many intimate levels. Almost every speaking engagement ends in a standing ovation. Even I am uplifted when in his audiences. In spite of the hurdles, we've grown even closer over the past four years.

Getting the "Pass with Care" amendment passed was very important to us. We never want another family to have to suffer through what we did. And we pray for the day Ford Motor Company will spend the $12 it takes to fix the gas tank on the Crown Victorias.

Mike is frantic that all his projects won't be completed before he dies. He's working way too many hours to do so. I have become the "Get Away" planner and I can't pull him off a project often enough. We cherish those times together. He admits he's flying through these months at Warp Speed. (I think it's faster.) I know a lot of it is just proving to himself that he can still bring some value to the table.

I hope that writing this book brings him peace. I hope that reading this book brings you comfort. I hope you will always believe after reading our story that God has a plan for each of us.

I didn't break down often, but one of the times I just couldn't cope was when he was in a coma, so damaged and so helpless. Next to the bed was the portrait of our family taken just three weeks earlier. Though impossible, I wanted to re-wind so badly and go back to that day. But this was to be a part of God's plan for that once-smiling bunch of Noltes. Acknowledging this made the process seem like progress and I found solace in the smallest of improvements.

My husband, the broad brushstroke man, "Mr. Type A+," is getting better. We are going to survive as a couple, as a family. Though his abilities were temporarily side tracked, his talents to impact people and help others are back in full swing. As a legion of people stand in amazement of his comeback, I stand in the wings and smile as I watch the way he touches people's lives. The way he touches their hearts. It's a very worthwhile endeavor and I'm proud of him. I'm proud and thankful to be married to such a man.

– Barbie Nolte

Back From the Brink

by Paul Anderson

August 15, 2003

On a mission of kindness,
For a friend who had died,
You got into your car,
And started your ride.

With thoughts of a funeral
Filling your head,
You had no idea
Of the fate up ahead.

How could you have known?
Any way, any how?
That too long on the left,
The law wouldn't allow.

With your friend on your mind
And a squad car in sight,
An eager young trooper
Pulled you off to the right.

As you sat in his front seat,
Perhaps cursing your luck,
The ill-fated car
Was about to be struck.

The impact was sudden.
The explosion immense.
The gas tank had ruptured.
The flames were intense.

You had no idea.
Armageddon? Or war?
You don't even know
How you passed through the door.

When you awoke,
Your faith took control.
The Act of Contrition
Would ready your soul.

The Lord's Prayer, the Rosary,
The copter blades twirled.
It was now up to God.
Would you stay in this world?

In the chopper you left us,
And you touched Heaven's door.
But the Lord sent you back
And you wonder, "What for?"

It might not be next week
Or next month or next year,
But sometime in the future,
God's intent will be clear.

With courage and strength,
You battled despair
For sixty-five days
In intensive care.

Through pain and through tears,
You offered it up.
You hungered and thirsted
For the Bread and the Cup.

You focused on Jesus
As He hung on the tree.
You would get through each hour
Because He gave us three.

The world is a better place,
I would think,
Since our Lord and Savior
Brought you back from the brink.

Matchbook testimonials: A little matchbook advice goes a long way. I had these printed and give them out whenever possible as a reminder to be safe.

To read more articles and hear one of Michael Nolte's speeches, visit **www.michaeljnolte.com.**

To contribute to the scholarship fund Michael has set up for the daughters of his rescuers and for Trooper Newton's son, contact:

Nolte Rescue Scholarship Foundation
5057 West 119th Street
Overland Park, KS 66209

To learn about Mike's professional life:
www.noltesbridal.com

Michael Nolte is represented by PowerHouse, LLC.
Visit www.powerhousenow.com